GUIDANCE FOR ADDRESSING

MALICIOUS CODE RISK

NATIONAL SECURITY AGENCY

9800 SAVAGE ROAD, SUITE 6755

FORT MEADE, MD 20755-6755

NSA-Guidance@missi.ncsc.mil

10 SEPTEMBER 2007

TABLE OF CONTENTS

LIST OF TABLES

LIST OF FIGURES

EXECUTIVE SUMMARY

The financial impact to the global economy resulting from malicious code is approaching the multi-billion-dollar range. Department of Defense (DoD) systems are not immune to malicious code, and precautions need to be taken to protect the information infrastructures, and ultimately the warfighter. It is in the best interest of the user to preempt the threat posed by malicious code, and thereby enhance the security of the system.

The purpose of this document is to provide guidance on safeguards that limit the introduction of malicious code into software and software systems in order to reduce the risk posed to software by malicious code. The intended audience for the information contained in this document includes system security engineers, as well as system and software developers, evaluators, and development program offices. To present this guidance effectively, it is presented in the context of various environmental characteristics and scenarios that represent different environments in which malicious code might be found. Key sections of the document include:

- *Environment Characteristics and Scenarios:* These portray certain important software characteristics and provide insights into potential security concerns associated with those characteristics. Environment characteristics include: network connectivity, the level and range of security domains supported by the environment, and the trustworthiness of the users of the system. Other areas of concern involve the criticality of the security functions being performed by the software (i.e. security-relevant or security-enforcing software) and the impact of the software's origin on system security and the software development process. Four environment scenarios are described that represent typical system-high and multi-level environments used by the DoD. Each scenario uses a combination of characteristics (i.e., network connectivity, security domain level, and user clearance) to reflect the security posture of the software being acquired or developed.

- *Malicious Code in the Software Life Cycle:* Discusses how malicious code can be inserted during both the acquisition and development of software. Provides guidance on reducing malicious code threats for custom-developed code units, acquired software components, or acquired together with custom-developed software.

- *Recommendations:* Restates guidance in a tabular format and maps it to each of the four scenarios. Breaks down the guidance into custom-developed software, pre-existing software where the source code is available for review, and pre-existing software where only the executable is available.

The remaining sections of the document provide the audience with suggestions on how to incorporate the guidance into realistic programmatic requirements. In addition, there is a section dedicated to various policies, standards, regulations, and other guidance that can be referenced as supplemental information.

A

1 BACKGROUND

1.1 TASK ORIGIN AND DRIVERS

The Systems Security Engineering (SSE) organization within the National Security Agency (NSA) Information Assurance Directorate (IAD) has a mission to provide Information Assurance (IA) guidance to the national security community and critical infrastructure providers to enable them to design, build, and operate secure information systems. With the growing trend in electronically interconnected information systems, such as the DoD's Global Information Grid (GIG), the risk to US Government information systems from malicious code is increasing dramatically. In recognition of this evolving threat, multiple system development programs have requested NSA IA guidance to assist them in mitigating the threat of malicious code.

The NSA Center for Assured Software (CAS) provides guidance and methodologies to ensure that software used within the DoD's critical systems is free of intentional or unintentional exploitable vulnerabilities. The CAS researches, develops, and uses tools and techniques in assessing the assurance level of software during production and evaluation. In some selected instances, the CAS will evaluate software for critical programs in DoD. The CAS also establishes or works to influence new standards and policies and educates users and developers.

This document was written by a cross-organizational Tiger Team that included participants from NSA's SSE organization, the NSA CAS, the Department of Homeland Security (DHS) Software Assurance Working Group, and the DoD/DHS Software Assurance Forum. The Tiger Team developed the IA guidance and coordinated it with applicable organizations, thereby providing a source document of IA guidance that could be tailored and applied appropriately to multiple system development programs. The Malicious Code Tiger Team began work in June 2006.

1.2 DOCUMENT CREATORS AND CONTRIBUTORS

The Malicious Code Tiger Team members responsible for authoring this document include:

- Dave Hoover, Information Systems Security Engineer (ISSE) for DoD Systems, Assistant Team Lead;

- Emmanuel Lewis, GIG Infrastructure ISSE;

- Joyce Lukowski, ISSE for DoD Systems, Team Lead;

- Larry Wagoner, CAS;

- Engineering representative from System Integration and Testing.

External contributors to the Malicious Code Tiger Team effort include:

- Karen Mercedes Goertzel, Booz Allen Hamilton;

- Participants in the Department of Homeland Security (DHS) Software Assurance Working Groups and the DoD/DHS Software Assurance Forum.

2 INTRODUCTION

2.1 PROBLEM STATEMENT

Currently, there is a lack of consistent guidance for reducing the risk of malicious code in the software life cycle of US Government systems. For example, programs initiating new software developments and acquisitions need to be aware of the threat of malicious code, and be equipped with ways to prevent the malicious code from exploiting their systems or circumventing their system safeguards. The goal of this document is to reduce the risk of malicious code in software with regards to confidentiality, integrity, and availability of the software and its data.

Often, blanket recommendations for mitigating malicious code in software are generalized, and are sometimes not effective for the various types of environments and characteristics of the system. For that reason, this document provides a set of scenarios that the reader can use as a guide for recommendations based on his or her particular scenario. Certain environmental characteristics increase the complexity of the recommendations; therefore the use of scenarios provides more effective recommendations for mitigating malicious code.

2.1.1 Definition of Malicious Code

For the purposes of this document, the definition for malicious code is taken from the Committee for National Security Systems (CNSS) Instruction 4009 *National Informational Assurance (IA) Glossary*. The definition states, "software or firmware intended to perform an unauthorized process that will have adverse impact on the confidentiality, integrity, or availability of an IS [Information System]." This definition is also used in the CAS Software Assurance Glossary. The definition includes the following:

- Unauthorized software that has an adverse effect;

- Authorized software that, when used improperly, has an adverse effect. This may include software in which exploitable faults have been intentionally included.

"Adverse effects" in this context include loss of confidentiality, integrity, availability, or another required property (e.g., usability, performance, reliability).

2.1.2 Understanding Threats to and Vulnerabilities of Software

Threats to software can occur at any point in the software life cycle. Because the risk to a system or piece of software comes from the likelihood that a particular threat will exploit a vulnerability, it is important to discuss the ways vulnerable software can affect the risks to the entire system.

There should be emphasis placed on the importance of secure design and development, as opposed to the practice of fixing security flaws after delivery. Security should not be tacked on to the end of a project, but rather integrated into the software life cycle as early as possible and throughout the life cycle to mitigate the threat of malicious code.

2.2 SCOPE

The primary scope of this document is to provide guidance on what safeguards and assurances should be used to reduce the risk of malicious code being inserted into software under development or in acquisition. However, even when all guidance is followed, a possibility still exists that malicious code could be present in software. Following this guidance will, at the least, make an adversary work harder and take more risks to mount a successful attack.

Malicious code can take many forms, depending on an attacker's motives, accessibility, and their risk tolerance for getting caught. An adversary may want to orchestrate an attack in a way that maintains plausible deniability should the attack be discovered. In such a case, an attacker may create the attack so that it masquerades as an unintentional vulnerability, such as a memory allocation flaw that enabled a buffer overflow or an intentionally weak implementation of a cryptographic system, so that, should it be discovered, the attacker can easily deny that the vulnerability was included on purpose. By contrast, it would be much more difficult for an attacker to disclaim responsibility for an attack such as a backdoor or trapdoor, a time bomb or logic bomb, or a Trojan horse.

Guidance will also be provided for reducing the risk of such malicious code as viruses and worms. Most viruses and worms are designed to be malicious, either by being destructive, by compromising information, or by enabling access to the host for malicious purposes. Non-malicious viruses and worms can be categorized as two types: benign or beneficial. Some viruses and worms are benign in their actions, either through design or implementation fault. Though they are benign, they still drain system resources through their activity. Alternatively, there are viruses and worms that are designed to be beneficial, such as by finding hosts vulnerable to a particular attack and then patching the vulnerability. Controlling the spread of a benign worm and perfecting it so that it does not unintentionally affect hosts adversely has been a long-standing problem with this idea. Therefore, all worms and viruses will be treated as undesirable, and guidance will focus on keeping them from affecting software.

Other software, such as key loggers and spyware/adware, may have legitimate purposes, yet can also contribute to an attack. However, frequently these types of software use some other form of malicious code as a delivery mechanism – in which case, defending against such entities as viruses and worms may also defend against the implanting of keyloggers and spyware. In most cases key loggers and spyware/adware are something to avoid, and guidance will be provided for these categories of code.

Several categories of malicious activity are beyond of the scope of this document:

- Social engineering activities such as phishing and pharming and in general Internet fraud are considered out of scope because their objective is the subversion of the behaviors of humans who interact with software, rather than the subversion of the software itself.

- Data mining may be assisted by executing code that has been surreptitiously inserted (such as spyware), but does not constitute a malicious code attack in and of itself. However, this guidance offers mitigation strategies for malicious code that might underlie the data mining.

- Easter Eggs are generally not malicious. If an Easter Egg is malicious, it should be categorized more appropriately according to the type of malicious logic it implements, such as a Trojan horse, time bomb, or logic bomb. This having been said, many software development organizations have policies that strictly ban the inclusion of Easter Eggs in software because they represent the inclusion of unspecified, undocumented features, which are a violation of security policy for software. In such a case, the presence of an Easter Egg indicates the failure to enforce security policy.

- Network issues or other system problems (e.g. instability, slow response, etc.) that indirectly result (as a byproduct) from the impact of a malicious code insertion or execution.

- Mobile code is a computing technology that is not inherently malicious. However, mobile code *can* be used as a delivery mechanism for malicious logic just as other non-malicious technologies, such as Uniform Resource Locator (URL) and eXtensible Markup Language (XML), can be subverted into mechanisms for embedding malicious Structured Query Language (SQL) or other command injections, or implementing cross-site scripting attacks. As noted in Section 7, Paragraph E.4 of Director of Central Intelligence Directive (DCID) 6/3, *Protecting Sensitive Compartmented Information within Information Systems—Manual*:

    > "Hostile mobile code or executable content is completely different from more traditional malicious code such as viruses and worms and is not currently detectable by conventional anti-viral software."

    However, mobile code logic that has itself been written to perform malicious functions can be considered the same as a similar attack that does not make use of mobile code technology, and therefore is addressed in this document.

The document also discusses various methods that can help confirm that code is secure. For example, Pass/Fail Testing can be used to check the validity and security of code and evaluation tools and verification techniques can be used when testing cannot be done, or is difficult or expensive to do.

2.2.1 Scope Expansion

There are many similarities in the mitigation strategies for malicious code and general software assurance guidance. To limit the scope of this document, only software assurance guidelines relevant to reducing the risk of malicious code will be covered. Similarly, this document focuses only on reducing or eliminating those vulnerabilities that could be exploited in software to enable insertion of malicious code. For example, since a buffer overflow in code could enable insertion of malicious code, recommendations in the guidance are provided to help prevent the occurrence of this exploitable vulnerability. Guidance for reducing the threat of malicious code in hardware and certain types of firmware were considered important topics, but are outside the scope of this document. The topic of network security itself warrants guidance however is also beyond the scope of this document. In cases where existing documents were identified that cover these out of scope topics, the documents were listed in the References section (see Appendix B).

2.3 UPDATE GUIDELINES

2.3.1 Corrections and Clarifications

Questions, comments and recommendations about this document may be addressed to: IA-Guidance@nsa.gov

2.3.2 Updates Required by Technological Evolution

Malicious code is constantly changing in its exploitation methods, taking on new forms, and creating new attacks. While the guidance gives some background into common categories of malicious code, it cannot account for all future attacks and methodologies. The guidance gives protection mechanisms that may prevent future attacks not specifically named in this document. However, the evolving nature of malicious code warrants updated guidance to account for future attacks and technology. This may be covered in a supplement or update to this document.

3 APPLICABILITY

3.1 AUTHORITY/POLICY

This document provides guidance in mitigating the threat of malicious code in systems developed by US Government and industry for use in National Security Systems. Given the threat of malicious code to the broader community, this guidance may be applicable to others in various agencies or private industry as well. In either case, this document is not an enforceable law, policy, or standard, but rather serves as a set of recommendations applicable to the environment scenarios provided within this document. The information contained in this document shall not supersede any existing policy for DoD systems. Implementations of this guidance may be combined with other policies and regulations as applicable to the user. NSA serves as the government focal point for information security in national security systems, and provides IA support to DoD components in order to assess the threats to, and vulnerabilities of, information technologies.

3.2 AUDIENCE

The intended audience for the information contained in this document includes system security engineers, as well as system and software developers, evaluators, and development program offices. The document provides guidance for the entire software life cycle; however, sections of the guidance may be more applicable to parties with specific security interests. For example, the document provides guidance for ensuring the security of software patches as well as guidance that helps to limit the effects of malicious code present in pre-existing software. The interested parties in these areas, which could include developers, operators, maintainers, and acquisition personnel, will all have different perspectives based on their mission functions, and would want to focus their attention to those particular parts of the guidance applicable to their mission.

4 GUIDANCE STRUCTURE

4.1 HOW TO READ THIS DOCUMENT

Because this document does not have to be read in its entirety and its intent is to present various sections that pertain to the interest of the target audiences, each section should be approached with the intention of determining how to apply it to the needs of the corresponding environment.

Sections 7, 8, and 9 are essential sections in light of this particular guidance. Section 7 defines a set of software scenarios that represents different environments in which the software resides within National Security Community systems. Describing the guidance in terms of these scenarios enables the guidance to be more specific to the types of problems encountered within these environments. Section 8 identifies threats from and mitigation strategies for malicious code in the software life cycle - from software inception through software retirement. The mitigation strategies documented in Section 8 are possible mitigations, but are not necessarily recommended for all scenarios in this document. Section 9 provides this document's recommendations, based on those mitigation strategies detailed in Section 8, for each of the environmental scenarios defined in section 7.

Section 10 offers recommendations on how to convert the guidance into program requirements. The final section provides definitions of supporting policies, standards, and regulations that pertain to the guidance. The final section also introduces additional documentation that includes some of the international, national, public, and DoD initiatives that address malicious code. This part of the document uses supporting documentation to incorporate some of the relating aspects into the guidance.

5 ASSUMPTIONS AND CONSTRAINTS

5.1 EXPLANATION OF "GOOD" ASSURANCE

This document is based on a number of assumptions and constraints. Those assumptions and constraints are described below, and should be reviewed to ensure that the guidance is appropriate and applied properly.

This document will discuss what is meant by "Good" assurance in regard to protection from malicious code being introduced into software during development, and also what is meant by building protections into software under development to minimize the effects of malicious code attacks.

This document provides guidance that will help developers and purchasers of software products to provide some measure of assurance as to the security of their system, but does not guarantee freedom from malicious code. In other words, the focus is on reasonable measures and workable solutions based on system developer needs and circumstances. In fact, this document recommends just such workable countermeasures to a variety of malicious code threats.

The user of this guidance should assume that commercial software and other non-custom-developed software have not been reviewed for security risks. As an example, open source software is frequently assumed to be secure because of its transparent development process and the open availability of the source, but may have security flaws that were not detected in functional review of the code.

Since there are a number of factors affecting the development process and the needs and limitations of the custom-developer, no assumptions on prioritization of security within programs are made. Security considerations as part of code development have, in the past, been neglected in the development process. Today, with greater reliance on software, security considerations must be part of the software life cycle. This document will recommend security activities and considerations in the life cycle that can both increase likelihood that presence of malicious code in software will be detected, and will reduce the opportunity for insertion of malicious code into software under development.

This document does not endorse any product or manufacturer. The document has been written under the assumption that most software, either custom-developed or pre-existing, can be vulnerable to malicious code, whether that code is embedded in the software during its development, or inserted during its production operation. The cost of securing such software should be taken into account, as it may be significant. There are instances when it is recommended that certain types of software not be used in high-risk environments.

6 TERMS AND DEFINITIONS

The following are key terms used throughout this document, and their definitions. Most definitions in this list come from the Center for Assured Software (CAS) Glossary.

Accountability
The property that ensures that the actions of an entity can be traced uniquely to the entity.

Adware
Software whose primary function is generating revenue by advertising targeted at the user of the computer on which the software resides.

Anomaly
Anything observed in the documentation or operation of software that deviates from expectations based on previously verified software products or reference documents.

Asset
Anything that has value (e.g. data, executing process) to a stakeholder (e.g. organization who owns it).

Assurance
Grounds for confidence that an entity meets its security objectives.

Availability
Timely, reliable access to data and information services for authorized users.

Property of data or software that ensures that it is operational at or above the minimum level of performance and accessible by all of its intended users.

Backdoor
Surreptitious mechanism used to circumvent security controls and provide access. Synonymous with trap door.

Buffer Overflow
An action in which more data is placed into a buffer or data holding area than the capacity that has been allocated by the system. Synonymous with buffer overrun.

Commercial Off the Shelf (COTS)
Software or hardware products developed and distributed by commercial suppliers. COTS software products are ready-made and made available for sale, lease, or license (usually for a fee) to the general public.

Confidentiality
Assurance that information is not disclosed to unauthorized individuals, processes, or devices. [CNSS4009]

Correctness

(1) The degree to which software is free from faults in its specification, design, and implementation. (2) The degree to which software, documentation, or other items meet specified requirements. (3) The degree to which software, documentation, or other items meet user needs and expectations, whether those needs/expectations are specified or not.

Custom-Developed Software
Newly developed software, most often for use in a specific system or application, where the government has control over its development. Contrast with "pre-existing software".

Denial of Service
Prevention of authorized access to a system resource or the delaying of system operations and functions.

Dependability
Integrating concept that encompasses the following attributes—reliability, safety, maintainability, integrity, availability. When addressing security, additional attributes have great prominence—confidentiality and accountability.

Error
The difference between a computed, observed, or measured value or condition and the true, specified, or theoretically correct value or condition.

Event
An occurrence of some specific data, situation, or activity.

Fail Safe
Pertaining to a system or component that automatically places itself in a safe operating mode in the event of a failure. See also fault secure and fault tolerance.

Fail Secure
Pertaining to a system or component that automatically places itself in a secure operating mode in the event of a failure.

Failure
The inability of a system or component to perform its required functions within specified performance requirements.

Fault
The adjudged or hypothesized cause of an error.

Government Off the Shelf (GOTS)
Software and hardware products that are developed by the technical staff of the government agency for which it is created or by an external entity, but with funding and specifications from the agency. Agencies can directly control all aspects of GOTS products.

High-Consequence Software
High-consequence software systems are those in which a failure could result in serious harm to a human being in the form of loss of life, physical injury or damage to health, loss of political

freedom, loss of financial well-being, or disastrous damage to the human's environment. Large-scale software systems that support a very large number of software users are also considered high-consequence because they are not only difficult to recover after a failure, but because it would be extremely difficult and/or expensive to make reparations to the affected humans for the damages that would result from such a failure. Examples of high-consequence software systems include the software elements of national security systems, medical control systems, banking systems, Supervisory Control And Data Acquisition (SCADA) systems for critical infrastructures, and electronic voting systems.

-ilities
Aspects or non-functional requirements. They are so-named because most of them end in "-ility." A subset of them (Reliability, Availability, Serviceability, Usability, and Installability) are together referred to as "RASUI".

Information Assurance
Protection and defense of information and information systems by ensuring their availability, integrity, authentication, confidentiality, and non-repudiation. These measures include providing for restoration of information systems by incorporating protection, detection, and reaction capabilities.

Integrity
Property of data or software that assures that it has not been altered or destroyed in an unauthorized manner.

Quality of an information system reflecting the logical correctness and reliability of the operating system; the logical completeness of the hardware and software implementing the protection mechanisms; and the consistency of the data structures and occurrence of the stored data. Note that, in a formal security mode, integrity is interpreted more narrowly to mean protection against unauthorized modification or destruction of information.

Justifiable Confidence
The actions, arguments, and evidence that collectively provide a basis for justified reduction in uncertainty.

Least Privilege
Principle requiring that each subject be granted the most restrictive set of privileges needed for the performance of that subject's authorized tasks. Application of this principle limits the damage that can result from accident, error, or unauthorized use of a component or system.

Logic Bomb
(1) Malicious software that will adversely affect systems under certain conditions such as at a certain time or upon receipt of a certain packet. (2) Resident computer program triggering an unauthorized act when particular states of an IS are realized.

Malicious Code, or Malware
Software or firmware intended to perform an unauthorized process that will have adverse impact on the confidentiality, integrity, availability or accountability of an information system. Also known as malicious software.

Modified Off the Shelf (MOTS)

A MOTS (either modified or modifiable off-the-shelf, depending on the context) whose code has been modified.

*OTS (Off the Shelf)

Existing software that is potentially available. Includes COTS, MOTS, and GOTS.

Penetration Testing

Security testing in which evaluators attempt to violate security properties of a system.

Pharming

A method of redirecting Internet traffic to a fake web site through domain spoofing.

Phishing

Tricking individuals into disclosing sensitive personal information through the use of e-mails that appear to originate from a trusted source.

Pre-Existing Software

An existing software component or software product that has been obtained for use rather than custom-developed (i.e., built "from scratch") for the system in which it will be used. Pre-existing software could be used as a "stand alone" application or service or could be integrated into a larger "pre-existing" or custom-developed system. Pre-existing software may be "off-the-shelf" (e.g., commercial off-the-shelf (COTS), government off-the-shelf (GOTS), modified off-the-shelf (MOTS), or any other variation of *OTS), "legacy", freeware, open source, or shareware.

Protection Profile

An implementation-independent set of security requirements for a category of IT products or systems that meet specific consumer needs.

Reliability

The ability of a system or component to perform its required functions correctly and predictably under stated conditions for a specified period of time.

Risk

The potential that a given threat will exploit vulnerabilities of an asset or group of assets and thereby cause harm to the organization. It is measured in terms of a combination of the probability of an event and its consequence. *[Source: ISO/IEC 13335-1:2005 Information technology—Security techniques—Management of information and communications technology security—Part 1: Concepts and models for information and communications technology security management]* Combination of the probability of an event and its consequence. *[Source: ISO/IEC Guide 73:2002 Risk management. Vocabulary. Guidelines for use in standards]*

Robustness

The degree to which a component or system can function correctly in the presence of invalid inputs or stressful environmental conditions, including those that are intentionally and maliciously created.

Rootkit
A set of tools designed to conceal an attacker and offer a backdoor after the attacker has compromised the machine. *[Source: Hoglund, Greg, and Gary McGraw.* Exploiting Software: How to break code. *Addison-Wesley, 2004]*

Security Critical Software
Software whose failure could have an impact on a system's security. See high-consequence software.

Secure Software
Software in which there is a high (though not absolute) level of justifiable confidence in the presence of a substantial set of explicit security properties and functionality, including all those required for its intended usage. For software to be secure it must avoid defects in its implementation that introduce vulnerabilities regardless of whether the majority of development involves either from-scratch coding or integration/assembly of acquired or reused software components.

Security
All aspects related to defining, achieving, and maintaining confidentiality, integrity, availability, non-repudiation, accountability and authenticity.

Security-Enforcing
Security-enforcing software is a portion of software that (based on system architecture) is responsible for enforcing the system security policy.

Security-Relevant
Security-relevant software is a portion of software that (based on system architecture) is not itself responsible for enforcing the system security policy, but is in a position to subvert the enforcement of it.

Software Acquisition
To obtain software development services or software products, whether by contract or by other means (e.g., downloading open source software from the Internet).

Software Assurance
The level of confidence that software is free of vulnerabilities, either intentionally or unintentionally designed or inserted during software's development and/or the entire software life cycle. *[There are a number of other definitions of Software Assurance. See http://en.wikipedia.org/wiki/Software_Assurance.]*

Spyware
Programs that observe and report on users; any technology that aids in gathering information about a person or organization without their knowledge.

Standards
An agreement among any number of organizations that defines certain characteristics, specification, or parameters related to a particular aspect of computer technology.

Subversion
Changing (process or) product so as to provide a means to compromise security.

Target of Evaluation
An IT product or system and its associated guidance documentation that is the subject of an evaluation.

Testing
Testing is an activity performed for evaluating product quality, and for improving it, by identifying defects and problems. The verification of behavior of a program on a finite set of test cases, suitably selected from the usually infinite executions domain, against the expected behavior. The five most prevalent types of software/system testing are: Penetration, Interoperability, Acceptance, Vulnerability, and Functionality.

Threat
A potential cause of an incident that may result in harm to a system or organization.

Any circumstance or event with the potential to adversely impact an Information System through unauthorized access, destruction, disclosure, modification of data, and/or denial of service.

Trojan Horse
Malicious program that masquerades as a benign application.

Trust
A relationship between two elements, a set of activities and a security policy in which element x trusts element y if and only if x has confidence that y will behave in a well defined way (with respect to the activities) that does not violate the given security policy.

Trustworthiness
An entity is considered trustworthy only when there is sufficient credible evidence leading one to believe that the entity will satisfy a set of given requirements.

Virus
Self-replicating, malicious code that attaches itself to an application program or other executable system component and leaves no obvious signs of its presence.

Vulnerability
A weakness in an asset or group of assets. An asset's weakness could allow it to be exploited and harmed by one or more threats. *[Source: ISO/IEC 13335-1:2004-11-15 (earlier draft of 13335-1:2005)]*

Watermarking
Process to embed information into software in a manner that makes it hard to remove by an adversary without damaging the software's functionality. Commonly referred to as "digital watermarking, or DWM".

Weakness

A weakness is an inadequacy in a portion of a computer system's hardware or software that makes that system susceptible to subversion, theft of information, or sabotage by an attacker. A weakness could be the result of an intentional or inadvertent flaw in the design, an error in the implementation, or an inadequacy in another aspect of the software life cycle process. If the weakness exists in one of the technological components of the system (e.g., an algorithm, a sequence of code, a configuration setting), and is exploitable by an attacker, the weakness is termed a vulnerability. However, not all weaknesses are vulnerabilities. Some weaknesses originate from inadequacies in non-technical aspects of the system, such as the system's requirements specification, security policy, or administrative or operating procedures.

Worm

A computer program that can run independently, can propagate a complete working version of itself onto other hosts on a network, and may consume computer resources destructively.

7 ENVIRONMENT SCENARIOS

This section is divided into the characteristics that define the environments and the descriptions of the systems. While these scenarios primarily refer to DoD systems, they are also applicable to the larger national security community as well.

7.1 SOFTWARE CHARACTERISTICS

When software is developed, its characteristics and the development process can have an impact on security. Likewise, the characteristics of the environment in which the software is used can have an impact on the overall security of the system. The following paragraphs identify certain important characteristics and provide insights into potential security concerns associated with them. These include:

- Environment characteristics such as network connectivity, the level and range of security domains supported by the environment, and the trustworthiness of the users of the system.

- The criticality of the security functions being performed by the software (i.e. security-relevant versus security-enforcing software).

- The impact of the software's origin on system security and the software development process.

7.1.1 Environment

The following represents some of the environmental considerations that can affect the security of a system. Each environmental concept is based on characteristics that define the system's usage. While these concepts are representative of systems and their environments, each can be tailored by the users of this guide to fit their unique needs.

Network Connectivity

The networks to which a National Security System (NSS) is connected can greatly affect the intensity of the threat to that software within the system. A stand-alone, air-gapped system does not need to be protected as rigorously as a system connected to the Internet because there is no way for an adversary to affect the system without direct or indirect physical access. An adversary cannot remotely attack a stand-alone system, and malicious information-gathering programs cannot export any information.

However, NSS systems are not limited to either being stand-alone or connected to the Internet; NSS hosts systems on NSS networks that operate at a wide range of sensitivity levels, from unclassified to Top Secret/SCI. Many of these networks contain information at various classification levels, some of which are mission-critical for DoD personnel, and some of which are multi-national coalition networks. In many cases, these networks are also connected to other networks. Each one of these networks presents different threat levels that must be taken into account when planning how best to protect software in such a system. The direction in which threats flow between a network and a system is not one-way, however. When a system is connected to a network, not only do all the other systems on that network present threats to it, but it also presents a threat to them. Coalition networks present an even more difficult challenge, as it may be difficult to determine what systems a network is connected to at the coalition partners' ends and thus, what level of threat is being assumed.

Security Domain Levels
The characteristics of the software described within this guidance are represented by the range of classification levels of data it processes. This guidance presents a categorization of environments based on the number of and interconnections between classification levels within a particular system.

Top Secret classification applies to information that would cause grave harm if compromised or destroyed. Secret information, if compromised, would cause serious harm. Top Secret is judged to be more valuable, both to the U.S. and to U.S. adversaries. This higher value means that it poses a more tempting target for adversaries' attacks. They only need to find one system vulnerability to exploit in order to breach the information's confidentiality, integrity, or availability of that information, while the U.S., as the defender, has to maintain security for the whole system at all times. For these reasons, both Secret and Top Secret information are protected, but Top Secret information is protected more rigorously. Similarly, Unclassified information, even Unclassified Sensitive Information, is not considered as valuable, and it is not protected to the same level of rigor as Secret information.

The classification levels within a particular system-high environment could range from Unclassified up to Top Secret/Sensitive Compartmented Information (SCI). In this environment, the information is all handled at the highest classification level for the environment. For example, a system handling Top Secret information could also contain Unclassified data, yet the environment is protected at the Top Secret level.

Multi-level systems include combinations of one or more classification levels within a single environment, and permit access by users with varying clearances so that they only access the data they are authorized to see. For example, environments can support classification levels from Unclassified to Secret, Secret/Special Access Required (SAR) systems to Top Secret, or from Unclassified to Top Secret. Users with a Secret clearance would be able to view Secret information but not Top Secret information. This type of categorization also considers the role that logically enforced data separation plays in the isolation of one classification level from another.

Software Users
Software users may be citizens of and located in the United States (US) or may be non-US citizens in other countries, such as citizens of countries that are partners in multi-national coalitions. A US user's clearance level may range from no clearance to Top Secret/SCI/multiple compartments. These differences translate into differing levels of trust. Higher clearances require greater vetting procedures which equate to higher levels of trustworthiness. When all users are trusted to the level of information processed by the environment, then the risk to the environment is lower (e.g. all Secret-cleared US citizens in a Secret US Only environment). When you have users that are not sufficiently trusted for all information in the environment, the risk is higher.

7.1.2 Security-Enforcing, Security-Relevant, and General

The stringency of the analysis needed to verify that a piece of code is not at high risk for a malicious code attack is determined by the extent to which that portion of software can affect the security of the system. If that portion of software (defined by the system architecture) is responsible for enforcing the system security policy, it is considered *security-enforcing*. If that portion of software is in a position to subvert the enforcement of the system security policy, but is not itself responsible for enforcing that policy, then it is considered *security-relevant*. Security-enforcing software should be examined rigorously, as it has the greatest ability to affect the security of the system. Security-relevant software can be examined less rigorously, but still should be examined to a level commensurate with its role in the system and its ability to cause harm, e.g., were malicious code to be present in it.

General software is neither security-enforcing nor security-relevant. Because it is not necessary to subject general software to stringent review, the system should contain mechanisms to isolate examined ("trusted") code from the general ("untrusted") code, so that the untrusted code cannot undermine the trusted code. The recommendations given in this document do not specifically address security threats in general software because, by definition, general software cannot affect the security policy of the system.

7.1.3 Software Origin

Most software used in the DoD is assembled in whole or in part from pre-existing components acquired from a variety of sources; these include COTS, GOTS, MOTS, and other variations of *OTS software components, as well as "legacy" components, freeware (the meaning of which can vary from product to product) and shareware components, and OSS components. Regardless of the origin (sometimes referred to as the *pedigree*) of a pre-existing component, an important consideration in selecting such software is how much knowledge the acquirer is able to gain about the component's developer, development process, and specification, design, and implementation details.

The ideal pre-existing component supplier will not only be forthcoming with details about the software's developers and development process, but will also make both source code and technical documentation available for review by the acquirer. Moreover, the supplier will have performed security checks throughout the software's development life cycle in order to verify the correctness and predictability of the required properties of the software (especially its dependability-related properties).

Unfortunately, most suppliers are not ideal when it comes to disclosing this kind of information to acquirers. This fact provides a good argument for custom development when a high level of scrutiny into the personnel, software development process, and resulting artifacts is desired.

Software that can only be acquired in executable (i.e., binary code) form with no provision for review of the source code is the most difficult to assure. Analyzing only the software's executable is made difficult by the lack of all but a few effective tools and techniques for "black box" testing (i.e., testing of binary code and executing software) and reverse engineering (in which binary is decompiled back into source code or disassembled back into assembler code for easier analysis). Because the acquirers of executable software are granted little or no visibility into or control over the process by which such software is developed, they are forced to place a large amount of not-necessarily-justifiable faith in the "goodness" of that unknown development process. In this document, such software is called *pre-existing with executable*.

In certain instances, pre-existing with executable software may have been reviewed by a recognized evaluation laboratory, such as the certification labs run by the National Information Assurance Partnership (NIAP) and National Institute of Standards and Technology (NIST). In the case of commercial (Type 3) cryptographic software, for example, a Federal Information Processing Standards (FIPS) evaluation would be required in compliance with national policy, during which the source code will have received a sufficient level of scrutiny to allow the acquirer of the executable software to consider it as having undergone a source code review albeit by a third party (in this case, NIST). "Sufficient level of scrutiny" implies that the third party applied a level of rigor in examining the source code, and looked for the same types of issues (e.g., hallmarks of malicious logic and vulnerabilities to malicious insertions) as recommended for code reviews in this document. Pre-existing with executable software that had undergone such a review process might be acceptable in situations in which use of pre-existing software with executable would otherwise not be recommended, provided that a trusted delivery mechanism was in place to ensure the software used was the evaluated version. In this example, the guidance for the software would fall into the "pre-existing with source" category (see below) because the "mitigation strategy" of a source code review will have been undertaken by the third party responsible for the software product's NIAP or NIST certification or evaluation. (Note that source code review is not included in NIAP Common Criteria evaluations for products at Evaluation Assurance Levels [EALs] lower than EAL4.)

Pre-existing with source software is software for which the source code is available. Often the software itself is physically obtained in already-compiled, executable form, but the fact that the source code is available for review gives the acquirer more options for analyzing the software than are available when the executable alone is available. Open source software, as its name implies, is software for which the source code is publicly available. In some situations, commercial vendors may also agree to provide source code for review under a memorandum of understanding and non-disclosure agreement. Some vendors also impose viewing constraints: for example, the acquirer can only review the source code at the vendor's location.

Even when source code is available, the acquirer has no control over its development process. Nor does the availability of source code always extend to other development artifacts, such as design documents, requirements specifications, and test results. If technical documentation is not made available, the source code analyst will be unable to gain a good understanding of the software's architecture and design; such an understanding makes it easier to figure out what is going on in the source code, and how the different code modules/units relate to and impact each other. Therefore, while analysis of pre-existing with source software is somewhat easier than analysis of pre-existing with executable software, without being able to check the development process or influence the developers to place a high priority on dependability and security, the level of justified confidence in the software cannot be as high as it is for custom-developed software (see below).

Custom-developed software is "written from scratch". The government has full control over and visibility (via audits) into the development process (either directly, i.e., when a government project manager directly oversees development, or through contractual and statement of work obligations). The government also has access to all software artifacts including the source code and technical documentation. However, this level of visibility and control come at a price: custom development is generally the most expensive way to obtain software. But for those applications and systems that have very high assurance requirements or other unique requirements that would be extremely difficult to satisfy through use of pre-existing software, custom development may be the best and indeed the only viable choice.

In summary, the three types of software discussed in this document are:

- *Pre-existing with executable:* Software that can only be acquired in executable (e.g., binary code) form, in which the acquirer does not gain access to source code;

- *Pre-existing with source:* Software for which the source code is available for review, even though the software itself may be obtained in pre-compiled, executable form;

- *Custom-developed:* Newly developed software, most often for use in a specific system or application, where the government has control over its development.

Even though these are seemingly distinct ways in which software could be obtained, reality is often not as straightforward. Custom-developed software and pre-existing with source components often use drivers, libraries, and other pre-existing software with executable. And the tools used to write, compile, debug, and test source code are all pre-existing often with executable only, so their influence on the security of the software may not be possible to determine. However, the intent of this three-types-of-software categorization is to provide a general basis for assurance of software. The less source code available for review, and the less visibility into and control of the development process, the more difficult it is to determine the assurance level for the software.

7.2 Scenario Descriptions

7.2.1 Scenarios

The following scenarios reflect typical categories of software used in the DoD. Each scenario uses a combination of three characteristics—(1) network connectivity, (2) security domain level, and (3) user clearances—to indicate the security posture of the software (whether acquired or custom-developed). Section 9 of this document maps the recommendations in Section 8 to each of these scenarios, breaking the recommendations down further by software origin (custom-developed, pre-existing with source, pre-existing with executable) and software type (security-enforcing, security-relevant).

The scenarios described below reflect four levels of risk, with Scenario A representing software at the lowest level of risk and Scenario D representing software at the highest level of risk. For example, exposing software that processes classified information to the Internet poses a threat that increases the overall risk of the system; such risk would need to be mitigated by applicable countermeasures. Risk, here, is defined as the likelihood that a threat will exploit a vulnerability. In this document, the exploits of most interest are those that are intended to insert malicious code into software, or to execute already-implanted malicious code.

While a system may contain data at more than one classification level, and be connected to more than one network, software or hardware protections can be applied that limit a particular piece of software within the system to processing only one level of data, or to connecting to only one external network. With such protections applied, such software would fit a scenario that reflects its limited connectivity and security domain processing. However, the software within the protection mechanisms would fit into a higher-risk scenario, as it is this software that bears the brunt of exposure to threats. In this way, the risk level of one software component may be altered by its relationship to another.

It is assumed that the appropriate cross-domain protection mechanisms are in place to adequately protect and separate the data when multiple security domain levels are present in the following scenarios.

The scenarios described in Sections 7.2.1.1-7.2.1.4 are provided in ascending order of risk.

Scenario A

Scenario A is the lowest risk scenario for which guidance is provided in this document. Software in Scenario A resides on a single-level network, which is a network or set of networks that operates at a single classification level. It operates in a single security domain, where all users are US citizens, and are cleared for the highest level of information present on the system or network, i.e. Secret system with Secret network connectivity, and Secret-cleared users; or Top Secret system with Top Secret network connectivity, and Top Secret-cleared users.

An example of Scenario A would be application software that processes Top Secret information within a system connected to the highly-controlled Top Secret Joint Worldwide Intelligence Communications System (JWICS). Each user accessing the JWICS must be cleared to the Top Secret level.

In the previous example, the software cannot be accessed by any unclassified networks, such as the Non-Classified IP Router Network (NIPRNet) or the Internet. Because of the limited network connectivity, single classification level of the networks and security domains, and the fact that all users are cleared US citizens, the malicious code threat to the software in this scenario is considered to be low-risk.

A summary of this scenario is included in the following table:

Scenario A	
Network Connectivity	Single level networks, no Internet/Unclassified networks
Security Domain Levels	Single level only
Users	Cleared to highest level of data, all US citizens

Scenario B

Scenario B is considered to be a medium risk scenario in this document. No network connectivity to Unclassified networks (i.e. NIPRNet or the Internet) is allowed in a Scenario B system. The software can process two levels of information that are at a higher level than Unclassified, and may be connected to networks at either of the classification levels processed by the system. Users must be cleared to at least the lowest level of data processed by the system. However, if a user is only cleared to the lowest level, he/she must be prevented from accessing the higher-level data handled by the software.

For example, a system that processes both Secret and Top Secret data, and is connected to both the SIPRNet and JWICS would be considered a Scenario B System. Users may be cleared Secret or Top Secret, but Secret-cleared users must be prevented from accessing Top Secret data. It is assumed that the appropriate cross-domain protection mechanisms are in place to adequately protect and separate the data when multiple security domain levels are used in this scenario.

Because there are no connections to Unclassified networks (including the Internet), Scenario B's risk is considered higher than Scenario A's, but lower than Scenario C's.

A summary of this scenario is included in the following table:

Scenario B	
Network Connectivity	Multi-level networks, no Internet/Unclassified networks
Security Domain Levels	Up to two levels of classification (e.g. S to TS)
Users	Cleared US citizens (access controlled based on clearance level)

Scenario C

Scenario C is considered to be a high-risk scenario in this document. Software in Scenario C has connectivity to networks at a broad range of sensitivity levels, from unclassified networks, such as the NIPRNet, up to classified networks, such as the SIPRNet, including multinational coalition networks. The software can process information ranging from Unclassified foreign-releasable to Top Secret. Scenario C users range from non-cleared to Top Secret-cleared. Users may or may not be US citizens.

For example, a system that processes tactical information will have both Unclassified data as well as Secret and Top Secret data. Both unclassified networks and classified networks are used in this system, including multinational coalition networks. Users, who may or may not be US citizens, are only permitted to access the data for which they are authorized. It is assumed that the appropriate cross-domain protection mechanisms are in place to adequately protect and separate the data when multiple security domain levels are used in this scenario.

Because coalition networks are not fully controlled by the US, it cannot always be determined who has access to those networks, nor to which foreign networks the coalition network has been connected. Therefore, the software in this scenario is considered high-risk because of the access by users without clearances, the connectivity to a loosely-controlled coalition network, and the Top Secret sensitivity of some of the information.

A summary of this scenario is included in the following table:

Scenario C	
Network Connectivity	Multi-level, multinational coalition, no Internet/Unclassified networks
Security Domain Levels	U to TS
Users	US citizens and multinationals, non-cleared to TS cleared, (access control based on clearance level)

Scenario D

Scenario D is the highest risk scenario described in this document. As in Scenario C, the software has connectivity to networks spanning a broad range of sensitivity levels, from Unclassified (including the Internet, NIPRNet, and multinational coalition networks) to selected Secret and Top Secret networks. The software can process information from Unclassified to Top Secret/SCI in multiple compartments (the most critical information in the system, protected at the highest level). Users can range from non-cleared to Top Secret/SCI-cleared.

Because the system and software described in this scenario is extremely complex and difficult to attain, it is not recommended in most cases. It is assumed that the appropriate cross-domain protection mechanisms are in place to adequately protect and separate the data when multiple security domain levels are used in this scenario.

Malicious code would have the most adverse effects on this scenario because of its access to non-protected networks, such as the Internet. Other risk factors include the extensive range of sensitivity levels of the data, and the access to the system or software by users without clearances.

A summary of this scenario is included in the following table:

Scenario D	
Network Connectivity	Multi-level, multinational coalition, Internet/Unclassified networks
Security Domain Levels	U to TS/SCI
Users	US citizens and multinationals, non-cleared to TS/SCI cleared, (access control based on clearance level)

7.2.2 Tailoring Scenarios to Fit a Given System

The scenarios described here are intended to represent common implementations of DoD systems, while the guidance in Sections 8 provides recommendations that are applicable to all software types and scenarios, as well as recommendations that are mapped, in Section 9, to each software type within each scenario.

Ultimately it is the owner or accreditor of the system and data that must determine the system's required level of protection against malicious code threats. These scenarios may be tailored as needed to accommodate systems that do not fit exactly within any of the predefined scenarios. System owners can select and combine recommendations from various scenarios to best mitigate the risks to software in their own systems.

8 MALICIOUS CODE IN THE SOFTWARE LIFE CYCLE

Malicious code can be inserted in software during its development, production and distribution, installation, operation, and maintenance. This is true whether the software is acquired (pre-existing) or custom-developed. From the perspective of this document, software is either acquired or custom-developed (most often by contractors, whose services must be acquired).

The current version of this document does not address the activities surrounding integration of custom-developed software units, the assembly of acquired software components, or the assembly and integration of acquired components with custom-developed components. Acquired software referred to in this document, then, refers to "turnkey" software that will be used "out of the box", and not individual components that will be integrated into larger software applications or systems.

From the point of view of the ultimate owner/operator of the system in which the software will be used, the life cycle for custom-developed software begins at the software (vs. systems) requirements phase, and continues through software design, software construction (coding), software testing, and finally installation and maintenance. The life cycle for acquired software (whether pre-existing with source or pre-existing with executable) begins with the acquisition phase, and then moves directly into the testing, installation, and maintenance phases. Both acquired and custom-developed software components are brought together during the testing phase of the life cycle ("testing" here refers to integrated system testing; code review and unit testing of individual custom-developed components is expected to occur during the construction phase). This notion of two parallel life cycles - one for custom-developed software, and another for pre-existing acquired software, is illustrated in Figure 1.

The nature of the processes for acquiring, developing, producing, distributing, installing, operating, and maintaining software can directly affect the likelihood that malicious code and/or intentional vulnerabilities can be embedded during the software's development and maintenance or inserted during its distribution and deployment and/or operation.

Software development processes should be "security enhanced" both (1) to counter the "insider threat", i.e., the rogue developer who embeds malicious code or exploitable vulnerabilities without detection, and (2) to engineer software that will be less susceptible to malicious code insertions and exploitation of known, possibly intentional vulnerabilities, during its operation.

Although such software development processes do not guarantee a secure software development process that will prevent insertion of malicious code by a rogue developer, such processes do provide for a series of reviews and configuration management practices that reduce the likelihood that malicious code insertions will go undetected by ensuring full accountability of all participants in a development project for all steps in the life cycle development process. Such processes also provide some protection against subversion and tampering.

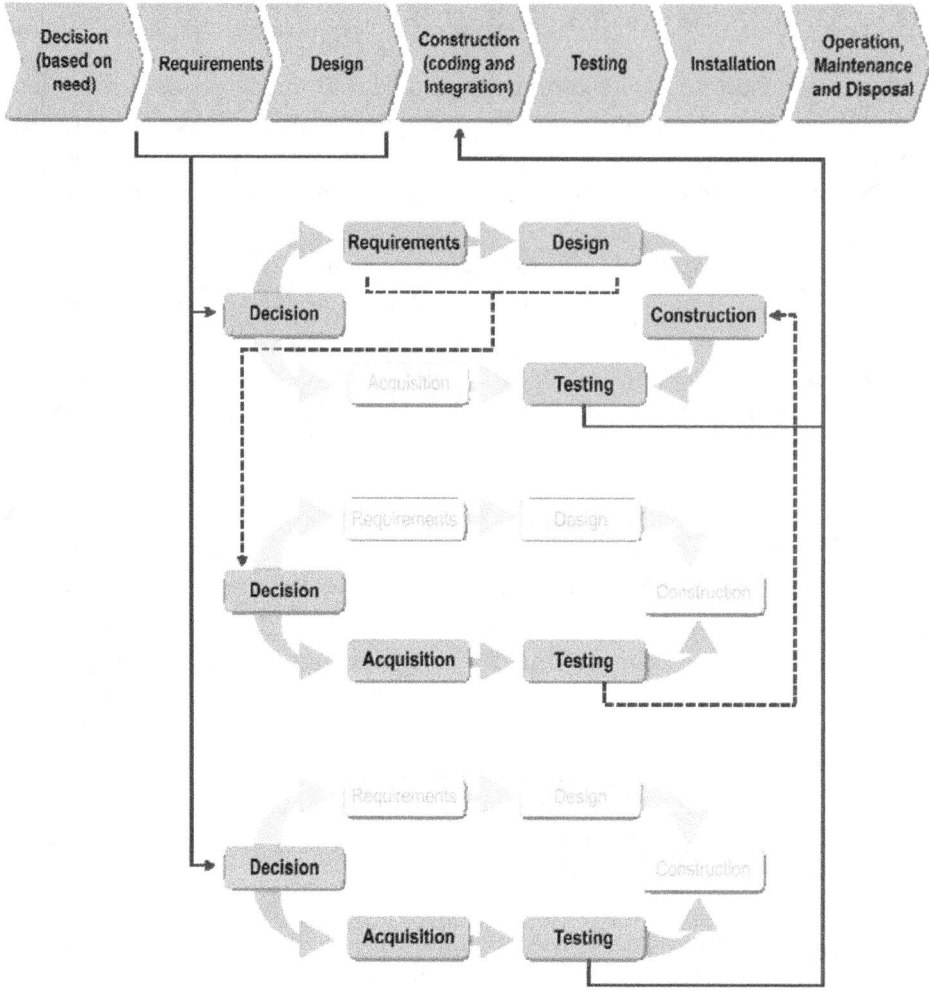

Figure 1: Software Life Cycle

The organization that develops the software (whether that organization is a supplier of pre-existing software or a contractor doing custom development) should follow a structured software development methodology the quality of which is audited and controlled according to a process improvement model. Ideally, both the methodology and process improvement model used will be open to "security enhancement" via the addition throughout the life cycle of iterative risk assessments, and security controls, criteria/objectives, reviews, and tests.

Software products developed specifically for the government should be produced in an environment that meets the standards for security that are appropriate to the software's status as security-enforcing or security-relevant. Reasonable precautions should be taken to maintain a secure working environment, wherein outsiders, including employees who are not working on the development project, are not allowed any access to the software artifacts under development.

Environmental control practices are described in Section 8.3.2.1, *Controlled Development Environment*. Personnel control practices are described in Section 8.3.2.2, *Trustworthy Developers and Developer Clearances*.

8.1 SECURE CONFIGURATION MANAGEMENT[1]

As described in National Computer Security Center Technical Guide 006 (NCSC-TG-006), *A Guide to Understanding Configuration Management in Trusted Systems* (known as the "Amber Book") and in Section B.2. of NIST SP-800-64, *Security Considerations in the Information System Development Life Cycle*, configuration management (CM) should establish mechanisms that help ensure software security, including:

- Increased accountability for the software by making its development activities more traceable;

- Impact analysis and control of changes to software and other development artifacts;

- Minimization of undesirable changes that may affect the security of the software.

By carefully tracking and controlling access to all artifacts of software development, secure CM helps ensure that all changes to those artifacts are made by authorized parties, and that they do not compromise the trustworthiness of the software as it transitions through each phase of the development process. Establishment of a configuration baseline for each development artifact captures the initial set of critical observations and data about the artifact for comparison with later versions. Such comparisons can help detect unauthorized substitutions or modifications. If every configuration item is checked into the CM system as a baseline before it is reviewed or tested, then as changes are made based on findings of the review/test, a new configuration item will be generated that can easily be compared against the pre-review/pre-test baseline to determine whether any of the changes introduced vulnerabilities (intentional or unintentional) or suspicious, potentially malicious, elements.

Unlike acquired software, custom-developed software is often developed by cleared developers in a controlled environment. Such developers are often allowed to exert a level of autonomy that would not be allowed to non-cleared developers in non-controlled environments. However, while the likelihood is low of a "rogue developer" appearing among cleared developers in a controlled environment, the software developed under such environments is also likely to be of significantly higher value, as is the potential damage if an insider threat against that software were to manifest. Because of the high value of such software, it represents a particularly attractive target to adversaries, who may attempt to suborn (or, through social engineering, mislead) even highly cleared developers, converting them into witting or unwitting insider threats. For this reason, diligent, secure configuration management and full accountability of developers should be maintained in *all* environments.

The CM system should enforce both separation of roles and separation of duties. The personnel who are granted access to the development, testing, or production environment should be assigned different, non-contiguous roles with separate access rights in the CM system. In practical terms, this will prevent developers from being able to access code that has entered the testing or production phase of the life cycle.

Within each life cycle phase, the developers and testers should be granted write/update privileges to only those software artifacts for which they have direct responsibility, and those privileges should be revoked once the artifacts have been reviewed, approved, and checked into the CM system. The CM system should require authorized users to authenticate themselves (e.g., using Public Key Infrastructure (PKI) certificates, biometrics, or usernames and passwords) before being allowed to check out or check in an artifact. The CM system should provide full auditing to maintain accountability of its users.

Software acquired or contracted from outside developers should adhere to the greatest possible extent to the relevant stipulations in the software acquisition policy.

8.2 CAPABILITY MATURITY MODELS AND SECURE SOFTWARE DEVELOPMENT

Currently, NSA recommends high assurance software developers implement the Software Engineering Institute (SEI) Capability Maturity Model-Integrated (CMMI®) Level 3 or higher software development processes. Adherence to CMMI Level 3 processes ensures full accountability for all steps in the life cycle development process and provides some protection against subversion and tampering.

Security enhancement of the software life cycle process is most easily achieved if that process already combines use of a process improvement model such as CMMI or ISO 15504 Software Process Improvement Capability (SPICE) with use of a structured development methodology, such as the Rational Unified Process (RUP), that is both consistent with the relevant processes in Institute of Electrical and Electronics Engineers (IEEE)/Electronic Industries Association (EIA) 12207 Software Life Cycle standard and includes peer reviews and/or tests (as appropriate) of each software artifact.

Although processes that adhere to CMMI, ISO 15504, and similar standards do not guarantee a secure software development process that will prevent insertion of malicious code by a rogue developer, such processes do provide for a series of reviews and configuration management practices that reduce the likelihood that malicious code insertions will go undetected by ensuring full accountability of all participants in a development project for all steps in the life cycle development process. Such processes also provide some protection against subversion and tampering.

8.3 SOFTWARE ACQUISITION

Given unlimited resources, software could be developed in-house, with its design and configuration custom-developed to the custom-developer's specific needs. However, in the interest of saving time and money, the majority of software systems are created by integrating pre-existing software components acquired from commercial vendors and open source distributions with a handful of custom-developed components.

A critical security objective for such software development projects is to ensure that the pre-existing components that are under consideration for use in the integrated software system will not introduce security threats or vulnerabilities into the system—or at the very least, that if such threats and vulnerabilities cannot be avoided, the software system is engineered in such a manner that the damage that ensues from the activation of a known threat or fault, or the exploitation of a known vulnerability, can be constrained and minimized.

During acquisition, then, it is imperative that security evaluation criteria be established and satisfied for all software obtained from commercial vendors or open source distributions. These criteria should include determinations that enable an intelligent, informed understanding of the level of risk that each acquired component poses to the system as a whole, including the risk that it may contain malicious code or vulnerabilities that have been intentionally inserted for exploitation when the software is executed.

Software acquisition should be tightly coordinated with the system's architectural design activities. The components to be acquired should be evaluated in light of the different design options possible for combining them in the most secure manner possible. The criteria for evaluating each pre-existing component should include "secure composability" criteria. If several components are available that satisfy the system's functional requirements, the component that is actually selected should not only satisfy the functional requirements, but should also be capable of being assembled with the other system components in the most secure manner possible. Secure development of component-based software is discussed extensively in the following references:

- Goertzel, Karen Mercedes, *et al* (for DHS National Cyber Security Division [NCSD]), *Security in the Software Lifecycle: Making Software Processes—and the Software Produced by Them—More Secure,* Section 3.5 and Appendix G:G.5. Draft Version 2.1, August 2006.

- Defense Information Systems Agency (DISA) Application Security Project. *Developer's Guide to Secure Use of Software Components.* Draft Version 3.0, October 2004.

8.3.1 Threats and Vulnerabilities in the Acquisition Phase

One indicator of a software component's likely trustworthiness is the trustworthiness of its supplier. Unfortunately, for most commodity software and virtually all open source software, the pedigree of the software is almost impossible to determine with any level of confidence. The nature of the global software industry is that implementation and maintenance of a large amount of commodity software, including that branded by major U.S. software companies, is done by those companies' subsidiaries or contractors located in countries in parts of the world where national economies render software engineering costs much lower than they are in the U.S. or the European Union. Moreover, many U.S. software houses claim to be unable to even determine how much or even which parts of their product lines are developed overseas. In some cases, their supply chains are so complex and convoluted that they truly do not know what is being developed in the U.S. and what is built abroad.

The safest course for acquirers is to consider all sources of pre-existing components, both commercial and open source, to be untrustworthy and potentially adversarial toward the acquirer unless proven (to an acceptable level of assurance) otherwise. Gaining a justifiable confidence in the trustworthiness of suppliers of pre-existing software is a challenge. Prior to attempting to determine their trustworthiness, the acquirer should determine how much trust in the supplier is needed based on the criticality of the functions performed by the acquired software (i.e. does the acquired software perform a security-enforcing or security relevant function). The more critical or sensitive the function performed by the acquired software, the more risk the software components pose, and the important the trustworthiness of their suppliers is understood.

While the use of commodity software can reduce the time and cost of developing software systems, secure use of such software requires increased due diligence on the part of the acquirer with respect to determining trustworthiness of software suppliers.

In many cases, the acquirer may have little or no insight beyond the reputation for security implementation of the company or open source organization from which the software is being acquired. However, when possible, assurance mechanisms beyond simply the contractor's reputation or organization should be considered.

Source code of commodity software may be poorly written and only scantly documented—both indications that the development and engineering management processes and practices of the company are poor. Poor development and engineering management tends to result in software that contains numerous faults, many of which can manifest as vulnerabilities when the software is executed.[2]

Although software consumers are increasingly requesting and even demanding that the products they acquire be secure, there is seldom any evidence to justify their confidence that the software's suppliers have reviewed and tested their products with security in mind. On the contrary, the inclusion of a plethora of features and conveniences typical in modern software products frequently runs counter to good security practices. By increasing the size and complexity of their software, commercial developers render thorough review and testing more difficult, and increase both the number of potential areas of the code that may contain exploitable faults and the overall attack surface of the product.

Many of the features of commodity software products are not needed or used when those products are integrated into a larger system. Such unused features should be carefully examined during security testing because they are unlikely to be examined during functional testing. Unused features and "dormant code" are two likely targets for malicious code insertions and vulnerability exploitations after the software has been deployed, because as areas of the system in which no activity is expected to occur, they are not paid attention to during normal system usage. Thus malicious code insertions and other exploits in those areas are likely to go undetected until it is too late.

Software is frequently designed to be able to run on multiple platforms. Because of this, alterations and compromises must be made in the software's design and implementation to accommodate the unique characteristics and idiosyncrasies of each platform, some of which may not provide adequate security services and protections or support the software's own security features adequately.

Software suppliers that cannot be determined to be sufficiently trustworthy may prove to be motivated by malicious or nefarious objectives such as intelligence gathering, sabotage, fraud, or theft on their own behalf, or on the behalf of an adversarial political or criminal entity. The software produced by such suppliers may contain exploitable vulnerabilities, undocumented features, malicious code, backdoors, and other weaknesses. Such malicious insertions may be made by a single rogue developer, or may be the product of an organized effort by a cadre of developers known or unknown to the software company. These developers may be on the company's payroll or may work under contract to the company. Even a company that does everything right in terms of its own software development processes and security checks may end up selling software that has been subverted by participants in its supply chain—a particular risk for companies that outsource development or obtain turnkey components from entities in politically hostile countries. Even software that has been thoroughly tested and approved for distribution by the supplier may be subverted during its distribution or deployment process, with the result that the software the acquirer obtains will not be the same as the software that was shipped by the supplier.

For software that will be used in systems that handle high-value assets or support critical missions, the ability to establish and sustain trust in the software's supplier is very important, as is the engineering of the system to minimize and constrain the impact of inadequately trustworthy (i.e., higher risk) components.

8.3.2 Mitigation Strategies for Acquirers of Software Products and Development Services

Foremost is the need to develop a security-aware acquisition policy for software and for contracted software development services. This policy needs to be widely publicized throughout the organization both to create awareness among employees and consistent enforcement of the policy, and the establishment of good security practices for acquisition. A security-aware acquisition policy should include the following imperatives:

- Software and development services should only be acquired from companies in which trust can be confidently established. Depending on the value of assets that will be put at risk through use of the software to be purchased or developed under contract, the level of due diligence required to determine the trustworthiness of the supplier or contractor may range from a simple background check, including review of the company's web site, "Googling" for comments on and reviews of the company's security track record, and a check of the DoD Computer Emergency Readiness Team (CERT), US CERT, NIST National Vulnerability Database, and similar web sites to determine the number, nature, and most importantly the company's response (in terms of effectiveness and timeliness) to discovered vulnerabilities in the current and previous releases of the software. When higher value assets may be put at risk, more in depth, involved background checks of the company's business practices, personnel, and international relationships should be conducted. Further, when contractors are hired to custom-develop software, the measures described in Sections 8.3.2.1 and 8.3.2.2 should be taken.

- The company producing the software should use a disciplined, repeatable software development process that is focused on producing secure software. Merely having a repeatable process does not guarantee that the software provided will not compromise security, as the repeatable process could be focused on delivery schedules or other criteria that tend to sacrifice security for other factors. A repeatable software development process allows an organization to use analysis of the quality and security of software produced as an impetus for improving the process. The background check of the software company should include a determination of the nature of the development process used in producing the software.

- There must be assurance that the product distributed or delivered by the company has not been altered between its final testing and its receipt (via download or on a physical electronic distribution medium) by the acquirer. There is little value to proper development and testing if the software is subsequently altered before it reaches the acquirer. Depending on the value of assets put at risk through use of the software, the level of due diligence in assuring that the software has not been tampered with after testing may be as minimal as ensuring it is downloaded from a known, reputable Web site or shipped on tamperproof physical media. As asset value or perceived risk increase, trusted distribution techniques such as application and verification of checksums or code signatures on the distributed software, out of band distribution of installation keys, encrypted delivery, and blind purchases may be required to reduce the likelihood of corruption or subversion of the software in its distribution to its acquirer.

- When acquiring pre-existing software, in accordance with national policy, the use of a NIAP or FIPS laboratory to evaluate the software at an appropriate level may mitigate the need to do some source code evaluations. Because of this, these evaluations, or equivalent evaluations done by trusted laboratories, may be used in place of stringent procedures or processes that are required for the development of custom-developed code. Acquired pre-existing software should be appropriately configured for security. Security Configuration Guides for various commercial products are available both through the NSA and from vendors.

Controlled Development Environment

Without strong controls on the development environment, the requirements and design specifications, source code, test reports, documentation, and other artifacts of the software development process that occurs in that environment cannot be trusted to be free from malicious content or influence. When specifications, source code, and test reports are being written, even if they are maintained under configuration control in a secure software configuration management (SCM) system, these controls may not be adequate to prevent someone with physical access to those artifacts from adding malicious logic to the design or malicious code to the code base. While the necessary privileges granted to the developer may make it difficult to prevent him/her, if she/he is a malicious insider, from inserting such malicious inclusions, many other people who might have physical access to the development environment should not be granted permissions or access rights that would enable them to edit the software's specifications or source code, or modify its test results.

Even within the development team, the role of the participant should make his/her access needs clear. For example, reviewers and testers may need read-only access to specifications and source code, but they do not need write-access that would allow them make changes.

The SCM system should have access controls as well as controls on its electronic interfaces strong enough to prevent malicious requirements from being added (or valid requirements from being deleted or changed) during the software's requirements phase, malicious logic being added (or valid logic from being deleted or changed) during the design phase, malicious code being inserted during the construction phase, and spurious results being inserted (or valid results being deleted or altered) in test reports produced during the testing phase. A development environment with an unprotected connection to the Internet provides yet another channel through which malicious tampering may occur or malicious code may be inserted.

The environment in which the software is developed should reflect the product's status as security-enforcing or security-relevant software. Reasonable precautions should be taken to maintain a secure working environment, such that employees who are not working on the project, as well as outsiders, would not have access to the development artifacts.

Access control of the development environment can be instituted either physically or logically, or both. In addition to physically limiting access to the areas in which the development systems and developers are located, physical isolation of the development environment would entail establishing an "air gap" by disconnecting the development systems from all external networks, including the Internet, though a standalone network may be set up within the physically isolated environment to enable members of the development team to collaborate more efficiently and electronically access the SCM system; logical isolation mechanisms, such as those described below, could be implemented on this standalone development network to help enforce Least Privilege, and Separation of Roles and Duties for all who had access to it.

Logical isolation of the development environment relies on electronic access controls and filtering mechanisms to limit the amount and types of data and artifacts that are allowed to pass to and from the development network, company Intranet, and Internet. These access controls will prohibit unauthorized changes to all development artifacts without the necessity of keeping the developers physically "locked away". While physical isolation of the development environment offers more security, it also causes greater inconvenience and higher operating costs to the development organization (and, ultimately, the government which is no doubt charged a higher rate for the development services when they must be performed under such conditions). The overall criticality of the system and the criticality of the functions performed by the software (i.e. security-enforcing, security-relevant, general) must be considered in determining what level of isolation is appropriate for the development environment.

Trustworthy Developers and Developer Clearances

For sensitive, mission critical, or otherwise high-consequence software, some level of background knowledge may be desirable to reduce the likelihood that the contracted engineers or commercial suppliers will include malicious code or intentional vulnerabilities in such software. Such development firms and suppliers should have reputations commensurate with the value (determined based, in part, on sensitivity and criticality) of the software to be developed. A company that has been in business for a reasonable period of time and has a reputation for providing useful and secure products is preferable to a company that is unknown. A company with whom the software development program office has worked on previous occasions, with satisfactory results, has an even greater level of trust.

When and where appropriate, personnel who work on software projects—including the software engineers, project managers, and configuration managers—should have the appropriate level of clearance. Software developed by cleared personnel, or vetted personnel without clearances, can increase the justified level of trust in those developers, and lower the risk that they will insert malicious code or intentional vulnerabilities. Developers of a single software component may not need to be cleared to the same level as the users of the system into which that component will be integrated, but some level of clearance can add assurance to the development process. At a minimum, personnel background checks should be performed to establish that the software organization's and team members' reputations are commensurate with the value of the software being developed.

Only trusted parties should have the ability to modify the development artifacts (specifications, code, test scenarios and results, etc.) at any point during the software's life cycle. These security measures will foster a system whereby any modifications of those development artifacts are traceable to the person responsible.

Each phase of the development life cycle should have traceability, meaning actions of developers can be audited, and transparency, meaning there is visibility into the actions of the developers. This helps to ensure that the process itself is not being compromised by a malicious actor.

This methodology can be augmented by reducing the amount of knowledge and responsibility given to any individual (i.e. Separation of Duties, Separation of Roles) throughout the life cycle. Equally important is the enforcement of Least Privilege, i.e., no individual should be given access rights or privileges that exceed those they specifically need in order to accomplish their role in the development process (i.e., capturing requirements, developing the design, writing the code, performing the tests).

All of these countermeasures will enhance the level of visibility throughout the development process, minimize the opportunities for a malicious insider to insert malicious code, and assist in the detection and attribution of any malicious activity that does occur.

Appendix G:G.3 of the DHS's *Security in the Software Life cycle* provides extensive information on secure design principles and techniques.

8.4 SOFTWARE REQUIREMENTS

Software requirements are specified by the developer at the beginning of the development process, based on the needs expressed by the software's intended custom-developer. The requirements describe the actions the software must perform to fulfill custom-developer needs. Security requirements should define the constraints that are imposed on how the software performs its actions, and express the non-functional properties required in the software, including its security properties (e.g., availability and integrity). Requirements may also be elicited from users. Other requirements derive from technological pre-commitments or policy and law.

Requirements, to be testable, must be written so they can be subject to a series of pass/fail tests. Security requirements are constraints on functionality or on non-functional properties or attributes. Expressing these requirements in a way that is actionable (and testable) by software developers can be a challenge. For example, the negative requirement that "no input from a user or the environment shall be allowed to cause the system to crash" must be revised into a set of positively stated functional requirements. Other verification techniques should be used when testing cannot be done, or is difficult or prohibitively expensive to do.

8.4.1 Threats and Vulnerabilities in the Requirements Phase

A significant threat to software during its requirements engineering is that developers will fail to capture non-functional and negative or constraint requirements, including those that will minimize the software's vulnerability to malicious code insertion during its execution. Such requirements are often overlooked because the users or custom-developers from whom requirements are elicited are either unaware of the need for such requirements, or take for granted that the software will be engineered in a way that will ensure it remains dependable even when it is attacked, is unsusceptible to malicious code insertions, and enforces appropriate security constraints on both users and processes that attempt to access the software's security-enforcing and security-relevant functions.

8.4.2 Mitigation Strategies for Requirements Analysts

Developers should not include features or capabilities in their software that do not directly map to documented requirements. Because users may not recognize that non-functional security requirements are necessary to ensure the software's dependability in hostile circumstances, the developer, during requirements elicitation, should do a risk assessment to assist in specifying adequate security requirements. The developer may do this by proactively proposing at least a minimal set of high-level security requirements (e.g., "the software must be able to detect and resist known attack patterns", "the software's functions must not be able to be altered during its execution", or "requirements should be implemented to partition or isolate general software functions from security-enforcing and security-relevant functions").

Once documented, functional and assurance requirements must be translated by the developer into detailed, actionable and testable positive functional requirements that accomplish the objectives of the original security constraint and non-functional requirements. The software's requirements review should verify that such requirement translations are complete and result in testable functional requirements. In addition, the reviewers should determine whether the requirements specification has adequately captured requirements derived from policy mandates or dictated by technological pre-commitments. Finally, the reviewers should verify that mandated or pre-commitment requirements do not conflict with user or custom-developer requirements, and that the security requirements do not conflict with the functional requirements. Whenever possible, conflicts should be resolved in favor of security.

Requirements specification should be carefully controlled by the CM process to minimize potential for unauthorized or undetected insertion, deletion, or modification of requirements by rogue developers. Once the finalized, approved version of the requirements specification has been checked into the CM system, write-privileges to the specification should be revoked for all developers until the specification next needs to be updated.

Appendix G:G.2 of DHS's *Security in the Software Life Cycle* provides extensive information on secure requirements engineering principles and techniques.

8.5 SOFTWARE DESIGN

The software's design phase is a critical point in the development life cycle for identifying and preventing potential threats and vulnerabilities and reducing risks associated with insertion of malicious code. As with requirements review, security must be explicitly considered when reviewing the software's architectural and detailed designs. This review should determine whether the design adequately achieves the objective of software resiliency in the face of threats that the constraint and non-functional security property requirements were intended to express.

The prevention and identification of vulnerabilities at this particular phase can reduce the creation of greater problems that originate during software design. During their "security push" in 2002, Microsoft observed that 50 percent of the security problems in their operating system, database, and Web server software originated at the design level.[3] With this in mind, the security implications of design choices must be fully considered to ensure that problems introduced at this earlier phase do not compromise the security of subsequent phases during software development.

8.5.1 Threats and Vulnerabilities in the Design Phase

The threat levels associated with software designs may be increased when the high-level design languages and tools used are inconsistent with or inadequate for addressing the software's requirements. Even when the requirements engineering and modeling methodologies used were security-focused, use of design languages and tools with known vulnerabilities makes it increasingly difficult to avoid the security problems that earlier-phase tools and methods were meant to prevent.

The software's design engineers are in an ideal position to maliciously alter the software's design. Despite the levels of protection governing this phase of the development process, malicious activity can still be performed by the very individuals with direct access to the software's design.

8.5.2 Mitigation Strategies

Designers

A key goal of both architectural and detailed designers is their ability to effectively minimize the potential damage to the system, its data, or its environment (in terms of extent and impact) that could result from execution of embedded or inserted malicious code or exploitation of "planted" vulnerabilities. In addition, the designers should minimize the exposure of known vulnerabilities throughout the software system. Designers should only be able to modify designs for which they are responsible.

Furthermore, the key objectives for detailed designs are simplicity and traceability. The former will enable the design to be effectively analyzed to ensure it contains no vulnerabilities or suspicious areas. The latter will make it easier to determine whether the design achieves the objectives, including the security objectives, documented in the requirements.

Design Tools

As with simplicity, high-level design languages and tools used should be reputable and understood by the designers who will use them. The languages and tools should have a traceable pedigree and provide a degree of confidence that their mechanisms can perform at a level consistent with secure design imperatives. To achieve a high level of assurance, especially for security-enforcing software, it may be preferable for the design tools to be custom-built, though this may significantly increase the overall cost of the software project.

8.6 SOFTWARE CONSTRUCTION

Software construction—coding and integration—is the software development phase in which the software is most vulnerable to malicious code insertions. While poor requirements and a poor design can lead to a product that is vulnerable to attack or subversion, it is during construction that malicious code or backdoors can be directly embedded into the software's source code, or malicious components such as keyloggers, spyware, or bots can be implanted.

Appendix G:G.4 and G.5 of the DHS's *Security in the Software Life cycle* provides extensive information on secure software construction principles and techniques.

8.6.1 Threats and Vulnerabilities in the Construction Phase

This following are categories of threats and vulnerabilities that commonly arise during the construction, as well as recommended countermeasures to those threats and vulnerabilities.

Escalation Attacks and Least Privilege

It is a common practice for system software to run with administrator or "root" privileges, even if that software does not perform any operations that require such elevated privileges. While this is not a directly exploitable vulnerability, it can increase the damage caused by the exploitation of other common vulnerabilities that enable an attacker or malicious code to seize those privileges. Many attacks have the specific objective of granting the attacker access to the system shell or command line, or of running the attacker's own code with elevated privileges. Should an attacker manage to subvert a process that runs with such privileges (e.g., via a common stack overflow [this type of attack and the vulnerabilities that enable it are discussed later in this section]), the attacker—or malicious code acting on the attacker's behalf—will obtain all of the privileges of the process that was subverted.

This threat is easily mitigated by designing processes to run with the lowest necessary privileges, and to relinquish those privileges as soon as the process no longer needs them. Moreover, application level processes should be designed so that they cannot possibly be used by an attacker to directly access (or "escape to") the system shell or command line.

Insecure Coding Practices

Many commonly-exploited vulnerabilities in software occur due to insecure coding practices. A programmer writing in a language such as C or C++ may invoke a function that is known to be vulnerable to buffer overflows, or may include functionality that was not part of the software design. Inclusion of undocumented features represents a major area of vulnerability, because undocumented code is an ideal place to implant logic bombs. Using normal (non-security focused) testing practices, such code never gets reviewed or tested. The potential for malicious code implantation alone is justification for adding security tests to the standard regimen of functional testing.

Even legitimate coding practices can cause vulnerabilities. For example, maintenance and debugging hooks that bypass security mechanisms in the software ease the development of software, but create significant exploitable vulnerabilities if they are not removed when the software is prepared for distribution. Software code review, Independent Validation and Verification (IV&V), and software evaluation tools will be very helpful in detecting problems in software that has already been coded.

Problematic Compilers and Libraries

Compilers convert higher-level programming language instructions into binary object code that a computer can directly interpret and execute. A poorly written or malicious compiler may change or add extra instructions, such as debugging hooks or back doors, or simply instructions with known vulnerabilities, during the compilation process.

Appendix G:G.4.1 of DHS *Security in the Software Life Cycle* describes how to determine whether standard compilers are safe to use, how to use them securely, and also describes secure compilers, runtime libraries, and other implementation tools that can help prevent vulnerabilities and malicious instruction insertions during code interpretation/compilation, linking, and runtime.

Dead Code

Dead—or unused—code refers to those portions of a program or component which are not executed when the program/component operates under normal or error conditions. Because this code cannot be reached from the normal entry point of the software, it seldom if ever gets tested.

Closely related to dead code is dormant code. This is code that is used infrequently during the normal operation of the module or component in which it appears, but which is not "dead", in that it is accessible from the module's or component's entry point. Dormant code is very likely to appear in pre-existing components in which only a subset of the total feature set is used in the system into which the component is integrated.

Exploitable vulnerabilities may exist (and may be intentionally planted) in dead and dormant code segments. Such code, if inadvertently executed, might cause the software to behave incorrectly, unpredictably, or to crash. Moreover, because they are seldom subjected to scrutiny or testing, such areas of software present ideal locations for the implantation of logic bombs.

The Code Review and Software Evaluation Tools sections below provide guidance on locating dead and dormant code.

8.6.2 Mitigation Strategies for Construction Phase Threats and Vulnerabilities

There are several strategies that can be implemented to mitigate threats and vulnerabilities during the software construction phase.

Code Review

Line-by-line review of source code is performed to identify dead or extraneous code, to detect code that does not perform its intended function, and to detect exploitable faults, vulnerabilities, and other weaknesses. Such reviews can also detect malicious code embedded in source code.

The performance of manual line-by-line code review can be extremely costly, in terms of required resources and time: most software programs contain millions of lines of code, making the cost of an exhaustive code review prohibitive. Moreover, reviewers of large software implementations frequently suffer from review fatigue: they begin the review process diligently, but after a few hundred lines, they may fail to detect problems, or may begin skipping segments, pages, and whole modules.

Line-by-line code review is best reserved for the portions of software that perform security-enforcing, security-relevant, or other trusted functions, the portions of untrusted software that perform sensitive or high-consequence functions but are considered at high risk of containing vulnerabilities or malicious insertions, and the portions of code that accept inputs from users or external processes. For example, if the code is written in C, C++, or another non-type-safe language, sections of that code that accept user input should be examined for possible format string and buffer overflow attack vulnerabilities. Manual line-by-line code review works best on small modules. Trusted functions should be performed by segments of code that are kept to a manageable size, allowing for intensive code review.

Tool-Based Software Evaluation

There are many commercial tools available that examine source code for common vulnerabilities and earmarks of malicious code. Such tools can ease the burden of a full line-by-line manual code review by catching some problems or flagging areas of code that are suspicious, and thus require manual investigation.

Such tools include those that examine the source code itself for sections which contain unusual or insecure coding practices, or which cannot be reached from the normal starting point of the program (dead code). Others examine code to identify high-risk sections, allowing the reviewers to concentrate their examinations more intensely in those sections.

Some Integrated Development Environments (IDEs) include automated or semi-automated code review tools and code checking compilers. Such tools are intended to assist the programmer (and code reviewers) by highlighting risky segments of code, such as calls to functions that are known to be susceptible to buffer overflow attacks. They can also be set to enforce a code formatting standard, making simple, inadvertent mistakes (such as typos) more obvious.

Tools can find many known programming errors that provide vulnerabilities in a fast and inexpensive manner. However, typically such static analysis tools will only find known vulnerabilities, and are not as effective in finding intentionally malicious code. Also, some of these tools produce many false alarms, meaning that an analyst still needs to go back to the code for review. While certain sections will still require a line by line code review, the effort required will be significantly less than if all source code was reviewed manually.

The NSA CAS and NIST's Software Assurance Metrics And Tool Evaluation (SAMATE) website may be consulted for information on code review tools and other software security testing tools.

Independent Validation and Verification of Software
Independent Validation and Verification (IV&V) is a critical element of the software development process. It provides for independent appraisal of the status of software development activities. Verification will answer the question "are you developing the software correctly?" while validation will answer the question "are you developing the correct software?" In addition, IV&V provides increased confidence that a quality software product will be produced. It does this by identifying and resolving problems in the specification, design, and code as early as possible in the development cycle. IV&V should include line-by-line code review.

The rigorous evaluation methodologies employed during IV&V for evaluating the correctness and quality of the software product can assist in detecting malicious code, thus increasing confidence that such code is not present. However, IV&V cannot *guarantee* that malicious code is absent. Nor, in fact, can any currently available technique or tool. As with all security problems, the best that can be achieved in terms of malicious code is mitigation to a level of acceptable risk.

8.7 SOFTWARE TESTING

As stated in the section on software requirements, software testing should be based on statements that lead to a set of Pass/Fail test procedures. A good model for procedures would be a "cook book" format that results in an expected outcome that results in a "Pass". If the expected outcome does not occur, a "Fail" is noted, along with a short statement describing the actual events. The tester does not suggest a reason for the failure or a fix. Tool-based evaluation and software verification techniques can be used when testing is impractical, difficult, or expensive.

8.7.1 Threats and Vulnerabilities in the Software Testing Phase

A number of threats and risks exist that can be detected by software testing. Tests can reveal known vulnerabilities in source code or binary executables. For example, tests can be designed to locate instances of inaccurate or improper memory allocation that prevent sufficient buffer space from being allocated to input accepting processes or lack of bounds checking before such processes write input to memory (both are memory management problems that can be exploited by attackers to cause buffer overflows). Be aware that testing and tools cannot check all possible instantiations that the code can create during its run, so it would be good to constantly observe code operation for anomalies in expected operation and provide security updates during the code operational lifetime. Dead code can provide "hooks" that can be exploited to insert malicious code. Viruses can be accidentally or deliberately inserted in the code. However, in spite of all checks and safeguards during software acquisition and development, there remains the possibility that malicious code embedded in software will go undetected during software testing.

8.7.2 Mitigation Strategies for Software Testers

Planning and scheduling security reviews and tests throughout the software's development is vitally important because malicious code can find its way into the system software at any stage in development and fielding.

Software testing is generally limited to functional testing, in which the software as implemented is tested to determine whether it fully satisfies its requirements. If the security requirements for the software are complete and thorough, functional testing should go a long way towards verifying the security of the system. However, even in situations in which software security requirements are deemed complete when the design of the software begins, because the threat environment in which the software will be deployed is constantly changing, it is impossible for the software's security requirements to ever be 100 per cent complete. For this reason, some amount of explicit risk-driven trade-offs should augment requirements-driven testing.

A regimen of rigorous security testing of individual source code and binary components, and of integrated software, should be performed. Test techniques such as penetration testing, security fault injection of binary executables and of source code with propagation analysis, fuzzy testing, and automated vulnerability scans should be used to augment functional testing, including functional testing of security-relevant functions. During testing, attention should be paid to the way in which the software behaves: Does it perform any unexpected functions? Does it perform its expected functions in unexpected ways? Do any functions take significantly longer to complete processing than they are expected to? If intentionally incorrect input is provided to the software, does it handle the error in the expected manner? Even if the software performs all of its required functions, unexpected behaviors, additional actions, performance slowdowns, incorrect error handling, and other anomalies should all be flagged and investigated as possible indicators of the presence of such malicious code.

There are various kinds of testers, who employ a number of different methods to their code testing. One form is software IV&V, which provides an independent review of the code by testers who are not part of the development team. Another useful testing method is to provide a group, different from the code writers yet still within the development team, to review each source code module to make sure that all compilation and runtime errors are caught, and that the compiled code runs correctly and produces the expected results. When changes are made to the code to correct problems detected during testing, all changed code should be subjected to recursion (regression) testing to ensure not only that the fixes work, but that the code still works as required with no new problems arising from the corrections.

Software evaluation tools can be used during code testing. There are two forms: static and dynamic. Static code assessment tools are used to test the code itself while it is not running. Dynamic code assessment tools test the compiled code as it runs while helping the tester trace different points of execution in the source code.

Evaluation tools can search for dead code, which, if determined to be a potential source of vulnerability, can then be removed. The threats associated with dead code, however, cannot be completely eliminated. Mitigation techniques that can be used to reduce threats are sound code development practices, and tool-based analysis of source code and binary executables.

Virus checkers are universally available, and one or more such checkers should be used to extensively check both code under development and code being evaluated for acquisition for presence of known viruses. The virus signature files of such tools should be kept rigorously up to date.

A port scanner is a tool that can be run on the test network after the code has been installed and executed, to make sure that unnecessary ports that could pose a risk have not been opened in the network firewall during the software's execution.

Another form of security evaluation is formal verification, which may be used in the software's design phase to mathematically prove the correctness of formal models of critical code (e.g., security-enforcing and security-relevant code), and again during the implementation phase to verify that the implemented software operates consistently with its formally-verified design.

In some cases, pre-existing software with source software needs to be tested for vulnerabilities through a variety of the methods described above. Code reviews of pre-existing with source software can find vulnerabilities even if 100 per cent of such code is not fully tested. The reviewed source code could then be recompiled by a trusted compiler to ensure that malicious code is not inserted by the compiler itself. Trusted compilers should also be used to compile custom-developed code.

Other methods of fulfilling the software testing recommendations in this document would include testing by an independent and established laboratory such as a NIAP or NIST FIPS lab (as appropriate for the type of software being tested). Even if the software development program office could not obtain source code from the supplier of the software, the software could still be considered "pre-existing with source" for the purposes of these recommendations if its source code had software that had been subjected to a sufficient level of scrutiny (as determined by the required level of mitigation recommended by this document) by the independent third party. This assumes that the acquirer is able to verify that the software received from the supplier is identical to the software tested by the independent third party.

Appendix G:G.6 of the DHS's *Security in the Software Life Cycle* provides extensive information on secure testing principles, techniques, and tools.

8.8 INSTALLATION (DELIVERY, DISTRIBUTION, INSTALLATION)

Delivering software to its intended destination introduces various threats and vulnerabilities. This phase of the life cycle includes software as it is distributed, deployed, and installed.

8.8.1 Threats and Vulnerabilities in the Software Installation Phase

The threat of malicious code can arise from the time the software is finished testing, up to the delivery time. During this period, malicious code could be inserted into the software through various means. For example, an attacker could intercept the software through the distribution mechanism (network connection for downloadable distributions, or digital media for physical distributions) and change or replace the software with malicious code, and then proceed to send the software to its destination.

A specific threat during the installation phase comes from improper or insecure installations of the software. If a person installing the software is not trusted, cleared appropriately, or simply ignorant of good installation practices, there is a risk of that person either intentionally or inadvertently installing malicious code along with the software, or of intentionally or inadvertently configuring the software so that it will be vulnerable to malicious code insertions during its operation. This threat applies equally to software loaded onto a user's workstation, a network or application server/service, or any other IT systems that performs an IA function.

8.8.2 Mitigation Strategies for Installers, Administrators, and Operators

Appropriate training of installers, administrators, operators, and end users can reduce many of the threats with regards to proper distribution, installation, and operation of the software.

To detect whether software on a physical medium has been tampered with, mechanisms such as tamper seals and protective packaging are used. These packaging methods may deter an adversary from altering or swapping the software.

Digital signatures, checksums, and digital watermarking are ways of enabling the software to carry evidence of its authenticity. Digital signatures, for example, can be validated to authenticate that the software comes from the expected, trusted source. This evidence should remain throughout the delivery, installation, and operational phases. Any changes to the software would cause the digital signature, checksum, or watermark to become invalid.[4]

Having only authorized persons send and receive the software through a process that includes a policy that promotes the integrity of the distribution process, such as that espoused by the Clark-Wilson model, and the separation of duties of those involved in the process is another mitigation strategy. Having a reliable means of transportation for delivery of the software is a countermeasure as well.

NSA National Computer Security Center (NCSC): *A Guide to Understanding Trusted Distribution in Trusted Systems* (NCSC-TG-008), provides extensive guidance on trusted distribution techniques for software delivered on physical media (rather than transmitted over a network).

Preparing software for distribution is an important activity, as it is the point at which a number of potentially dangerous inclusions in software must be eliminated before the software is fielded.

The DHS's *Security in the Software Life Cycle*, Appendix G:G.7, also provides extensive information on how to prepare software for distribution and how to distribute it securely.

When software is installed and configured, several precautions can be implemented for protection from malicious code or a vulnerable configuration which malicious code can exploit. One such precaution is installation documentation that is thorough and stresses the use of secure procedures for installation and configuration of the software and components. For example, all software should be configured to the same levels of restriction in which they were tested. The installation procedure can then focus on how to reset the few default configuration restrictions that must be relaxed in order for the software to function correctly in its target environment, rather than how to "lock down" vulnerable software after it has been installed. Security configuration guides available through NSA's webpage, www.nsa.gov, provide additional help for secure installation. Another example is allowing only authorized administrators to grant approval for installations of patches and software updates that maintain the security of the software.[5] Increasing the level of trust in the people who perform software installation and configuration may reduce the risk of poor or malicious installations.

8.9 SOFTWARE MAINTENANCE: OPERATION, MAINTENANCE, AND DISPOSAL

After software is installed, it enters the software maintenance phase. This phase of the life cycle comprises three sub-phases: Operation, Maintenance, and Disposal. Operation includes the activities performed to keep the software running effectively in its live environment as a service to its users. Maintenance comprises the activities of the organization that maintains the software. This includes managing modifications to the software to keep it current and in operational fitness. The Operation and Maintenance activities usually occur in parallel. The final phase is the Disposal phase. Disposal includes the migration and retirement of the software.[6]

Malicious code poses a threat to the software during this phase of the life cycle, so it is important to implement appropriate security mechanisms to counter this threat while in use.

8.9.1 Threats and Vulnerabilities in the Software Maintenance Phase

Some malicious code threats during the software's operation include attacks intended to implant new malicious code or to execute a vulnerability or malicious code embedded in the targeted software. Examples of these attacks include zero-day attacks; viruses (macro, polymorphic, stealth viruses); worms; logic and time bombs; Trojan horses; network attacks; exploitation of trapdoors and rootkits; cross-site scripting attacks; SQL, XML, and other command injection attacks; exploitation of buffer overflows; format-string attacks; insider attacks; malicious mobile code attacks and reconnaissance attacks such as connection or password sniffing.

Malicious code vulnerabilities are introduced during maintenance of the software, just as when the software was constructed. Downloading recommended security patches is considered to be a best practice; however certain patches may have adverse effects. For example, some patches may be compromised, or have inadequate testing and validation. Patches may also conflict with environment components as they are configured in the operational environment. Obtaining patches or updates from multiple sources may increase the vulnerability of the software; this is especially true for systems that also contain OSS or legacy components. Network stability and regression issues may occur, or patches may interfere adversely with the previously existing software.

The disposal of software introduces various malicious code threats. For example, software has varying life spans, and old and unsupported versions may become vulnerable to a future attack if not altered or retired. Unsupported software, including legacy software, may be vulnerable if a new attack surfaces, because of its lack of having a patch or update ready for use.

8.9.2 Mitigation Strategies for Operators and Maintainers

A layered approach to security can significantly reduce the vulnerability of fielded software to malicious code attacks. Because there isn't a single solution to securing software, multiple countermeasures can be used to provide greater assurance. A combination of countermeasures can be used to collectively block suspicious input, detect malicious code insertions, and constrain and isolate executing malicious code to prevent its propagation or widespread damage. These countermeasures include malicious code scanning products, electronic security (access control countermeasures and virtual machine/sandboxes), trapdoor access constraints (trusted administrators, personnel security), network security, connection and password sniffing countermeasures, application layer firewalls and security gateways, and physical security measures.[7]

Continuous monitoring of software is a way to detect malicious code intending to compromise the software, or to detect software that has already been compromised. There are various methods to perform the monitoring, depending on the type of system and the environment. Intrusion detection systems facilitate this kind of monitoring. They can be network or host based, and signature or anomaly based. Intrusion Prevention systems are designed to intercept and prevent hostile packets from continuing into the network and doing damage, which also use signature- and anomaly-based methods.[8]

Anti-virus software that is kept up to date can detect and expose known patterns of viruses and worms. Sometimes a virus that is not known, and therefore doesn't have a signature, can still be detected because of the similarities it shares with other known viruses.[9] Other tools such as heuristic scanners, firewalls, filters, and integrity checkers are useful in the detection of malicious code.

Depending on the network connections of the system, policies about scanning outside media and software may be put in place for added security.

Installation of patches and software updates are important security mechanisms for operational software. Maintaining software patches and updates helps to prevent unauthorized users from exploiting weaknesses in the software. The use of these patches and updates should be used appropriately for the software's environment, as there can be drawbacks and security risks when patches are not implemented properly.

Because software patches and updates are so important to the software, implementation of a patch management process is one way to strengthen the software's security. There are various guidelines available that can be tailored to an individual environment, but generally they include some or all of the following:

- A policy or strategy should be tailored to the system's unique environment.

- A team of qualified and trained individuals should be responsible for overseeing and implementing the process.

- Appropriate testing should be done to ensure that the patch is applied appropriately to the intended environment. As different patches and updates are released, it is important to maintain control over which ones are implemented through a version control process.

- A process for removing patches and updates should also be developed. In the event that a patch has an adverse effect, procedures can facilitate the removal of such software.

- Vulnerabilities should be patched in a timely manner. Version control and configuration control should be used in the event of an issue with the patch or update.

- Patches should be deployed on the least sensitive or critical software first, in the event that the software fails.[10]

- Continuous monitoring of the software should be done on a regular basis. Patch maintenance should be an ongoing process, with regular reports and logs.[11]

- Patches should be examined for the presence of malicious code in a manner equivalent to the level at which the software being patched was examined.

Verification of patches and adequate testing within the patch management process can deter many of these effects. Patches should be obtained through authorized channels, in accordance with policy. The use of digital signatures on patches from trusted sources can provide authentication of the source and integrity of the patch.

Implementing an incident response policy is a way to streamline the recovery process from a malicious code attack. A policy usually has procedures for detection of the threat, response to the threat, and recovery of the affected services (i.e. hardware, software, data, and connectivity).

Educating users and developers on the various threats of malicious code is also a countermeasure. This can be done through employee awareness training.

Disposal of software can eliminate the vulnerability of having unsupported software, which may have security vulnerabilities.

Appendix G:G.8 of the DHS's *Security in the Software Life Cycle* provides extensive information on maintaining the security of software after its deployment.

Guidance for Addressing Malicious Code Risk

9 RECOMMENDATIONS

The following charts provide tailored mitigation strategies from Section 8 for each Scenario from Section 7. Section 9.1 provides guidance for all of the scenarios, as each mitigation strategy in the table is applicable to all of the scenarios in Section 7. Sections 9.2-9.5 are tailored for the individual scenarios. It is important to document the history of flaws, vulnerabilities, and mitigation strategies to enable more accurate risk assessments.

9.1 GUIDANCE FOR ALL SCENARIOS

The guidance in Table 9-1 is derived from Section 8, and applies to all Scenarios.

Table 9-1: Guidance for All Scenarios

Source of Guidance (document section)	Guidance
8.1. Configuration Management	Apply secure configuration management to all code
8.4. Requirements	Safeguard tools to prevent alteration Actionable, unambiguous requirements Testable (pass/fail) requirements Include security requirements
8.8. Installation	Appropriate training of users and administrators Appropriate installers (i.e., patch installation) Thorough installation documentation Documented and authorized distribution (reliable transportation)
8.9. Maintenance	Layered approach to security Continuous monitoring (IDS, etc.) Tools (anti-virus, scanners, data integrity tools, firewalls, filters) Patch Management process Incident response policy Employee awareness training Proper disposal of software

Guidance for Addressing Malicious Code Risk

9.2 GUIDANCE FOR SCENARIO A

The guidance in Table 9-2 is derived from Section 8, and applies to Scenario A.

Table 9-2: Guidance for Scenario A

| | **SECURITY-ENFORCING SOFTWARE** | | |
	Custom-developed	**Pre-existing with Source**	**Pre-existing with Executable**
Acquisition	Trustworthy developers (contractor reputation)	NIAP or FIPS evaluation Acquisition Policy, including: • Background checks on developer/supplier • Trusted distribution (checksums, signatures, authenticated out of band distribution channel) • Blind buys	NIAP or FIPS evaluation Acquisition Policy, including: • Background checks on developer/supplier • Trusted distribution (checksums, signatures, authenticated out of band distribution channel) • Blind buys
Design	Separation of duties: Designers modify only parts for which they're responsible Reputable, well-understood high-level design languages and tools. Least Privilege/Fail Secure Design	n/a	n/a
Construction	Separation of duties: Coders modify only code for which they're responsible Software evaluation tools Code review	n/a	n/a
Testing	Software evaluation tools Security testing to ensure security requirements are fulfilled. Inter-team Testing	Software evaluation tools Security testing to ensure security requirements are fulfilled. Inter-team Testing	Software evaluation tools Security testing to ensure security requirements are fulfilled.

| | Custom-developed | SECURITY-RELEVANT SOFTWARE | |
		Pre-existing with Source	Pre-existing with Executable
Acquisition	Trustworthy developers (contractor reputation)	Acquisition Policy, including: • Background checks on developer/supplier • Trusted distribution (checksums, signatures, authenticated out of band distribution channel) • Blind buys	NIAP or FIPS evaluation, *OR* Acquisition Policy, including: • Background checks on developer/supplier • Trusted distribution (checksums, signatures, authenticated out of band distribution channel) • Blind buys
Design	Separation of duties: Designers modify only parts for which they're responsible Reputable, well-understood high-level design languages and tools.	n/a	n/a
Construction	Separation of duties: Coders modify only code for which they're responsible Software evaluation tools Code review	n/a	n/a
Testing	Software evaluation tools	Software evaluation tools	Software evaluation tools

Guidance for Addressing Malicious Code Risk

9.3 GUIDANCE FOR SCENARIO B

The guidance in Table 9-3 is derived from Section 8, and applies to Scenario B.

Table 9-3: Guidance for Scenario B

	Custom-developed	SECURITY-ENFORCING SOFTWARE Pre-existing with Source	Pre-existing with Executable
Acquisition	Background checks on developers Trustworthy developers (contractor reputation) Contractor has attained CMMI Level 3 certification or equivalent Logically-closed development environment	NIAP or FIPS evaluation Acquisition Policy, including: • Background checks on developer/ supplier • Trusted distribution (checksums, signatures, authenticated out of band distribution channel) • Blind buys	NIAP or FIPS evaluation Acquisition Policy, including: • Background checks on developer/ supplier • Trusted distribution (checksums, signatures, authenticated out of band distribution channel) • Blind buys
Design	Separation of duties: Designers modify only parts for which they're responsible Reputable, well-understood high-level design languages and tools. Least Privilege/Fail Secure Design	n/a	n/a
Construction	Separation of duties: Coders modify only code for which they're responsible Software evaluation tools Code review	n/a	n/a
Testing	Software evaluation tools Security testing to ensure security requirements are fulfilled. IV&V	Software evaluation tools Security testing to ensure security requirements are fulfilled. Judicious line-by-line code review	Software evaluation tools Security testing to ensure security requirements are fulfilled. Penetration testing

Guidance for Addressing Malicious Code Risk

SECURITY-ENFORCING SOFTWARE cont'd			
	Custom-developed	**Pre-existing with Source**	**Pre-existing with Executable**
Installation	Digital protection mechanisms (digital signatures, checksums, digital watermarks)	Digital protection mechanisms (digital signatures, checksums, digital watermarks)	Digital protection mechanisms (digital signatures, checksums, digital watermarks)

SECURITY-RELEVANT SOFTWARE			
	Custom-developed	**Pre-existing with Source**	**Pre-existing with Executable**
Acquisition	Trustworthy developers (contractor reputation)	Acquisition Policy, including: • Background checks on developer/ supplier • Trusted distribution (checksums, signatures, authenticated out of band distribution channel) • Blind buys	NIAP or FIPS evaluation, *OR* Acquisition Policy, including: • Background checks on developer/ supplier • Trusted distribution (checksums, signatures, authenticated out of band distribution channel) • Blind buys
Design	Separation of duties: Designers modify only parts for which they're responsible Reputable, well-understood high-level design languages and tools.	n/a	n/a
Construction	Separation of duties: Coders modify only code for which they're responsible Software evaluation tools Code review	n/a	n/a

	SECURITY-RELEVANT SOFTWARE cont'd		
	Custom-developed	Pre-existing with Source	Pre-existing with Executable
Testing	Software evaluation tools	Software evaluation tools	Software evaluation tools

Guidance for Addressing Malicious Code Risk

9.4 GUIDANCE FOR SCENARIO C

The guidance in Table 9-4 is derived from Section 8, and applies to Scenario C.

Table 9-4: Guidance for Scenario C

		SECURITY-ENFORCING SOFTWARE	
	Custom-developed	**Pre-existing with Source**	**Pre-existing with Executable**
Acquisition	Clearances for developers Trustworthy developers (contractor reputation) Contractor has attained CMMI Level 3 certification or equivalent Logically-closed development environment	NIAP or FIPS evaluation Acquisition Policy, including: • Background checks on developer/ supplier • Trusted distribution (checksums, signatures, authenticated out of band distribution channel) • Blind buys	Not recommended *(There may be exceptions based on evaluated software conditions. For such exceptions, apply guidance for "pre-existing with source".)*
Design	Separation of duties: Designers modify only parts for which they're responsible Reputable, well-understood high-level design languages and tools. Least Privilege/Fail Secure Design	n/a	n/a
Construction	Separation of duties: Coders modify only code for which they're responsible Software evaluation tools Trustworthy compilers Code review	n/a	n/a

SECURITY-ENFORCING SOFTWARE cont'd

	Custom-developed	Pre-existing with Source	Pre-existing with Executable
Testing	IV&V Software evaluation tools Security testing to ensure security requirements are fulfilled. Judicious line-by-line code review Penetration testing	Software evaluation tools Security testing to ensure security requirements are fulfilled. Judicious line-by-line code review Penetration testing	n/a
Installation	Digital protection mechanisms (digital signatures, checksums, digital watermarks) Anti-tamper mechanisms (e.g., anti-tamper seals)	Digital protection mechanisms (digital signatures, checksums, digital watermarks) Anti-tamper mechanisms (e.g., anti-tamper seals)	n/a

SECURITY-RELEVANT SOFTWARE

	Custom-developed	Pre-existing with Source	Pre-existing with Executable
Acquisition	Trustworthy developers (contractor reputation) Contractor has attained CMMI Level 3 certification or equivalent Logically-closed development environment	Acquisition Policy, including: • Background checks on developer/supplier • Trusted distribution (checksums, signatures, authenticated out of band distribution channel) • Blind buys	NIAP or FIPS evaluation, *OR* Acquisition Policy, including: • Background checks on developer/supplier • Trusted distribution (checksums, signatures, authenticated out of band distribution channel) • Blind buys

		SECURITY-RELEVANT SOFTWARE cont'd	
	Custom-developed	Pre-existing with Source	Pre-existing with Executable
Design	Separation of duties: Designers modify only parts for which they're responsible Reputable, well-understood high-level design languages and tools.	n/a	n/a
Construction	Separation of duties: Coders modify only code for which they're responsible Software evaluation tools Code review	n/a	n/a
Testing	Security testing to ensure security requirements are fulfilled Software evaluation tools	Security testing to ensure security requirements are fulfilled Software evaluation tools	Security testing to ensure security requirements are fulfilled Software evaluation tools
Installation	Digital protection mechanisms (digital signatures, checksums, digital watermarks)	Digital protection mechanisms (digital signatures, checksums, digital watermarks)	Digital protection mechanisms (digital signatures, checksums, digital watermarks)

9.5 GUIDANCE FOR SCENARIO D

The guidance in Table 9-5 is derived from Section 8, and applies to Scenario D.

Table 9-5: Guidance for Scenario D

	SECURITY-ENFORCING SOFTWARE		
	Custom-developed	Pre-existing with Source	Pre-existing with Executable
Acquisition	Clearances for developers Trustworthy developers (contractor reputation) Contractor has attained CMMI Level 3 certification or equivalent Physically-closed development environment	NIAP or FIPS evaluation Acquisition Policy, including: • Background checks on developer/supplier • Trusted distribution (checksums, signatures, authenticated out of band distribution channel) • Blind buys	Not recommended *(There may be exceptions based on evaluated software conditions. For such exceptions, apply guidance for "pre-existing with source".)*
Design	Separation of duties: Designers modify only parts for which they're responsible Reputable, well-understood high-level design languages and tools. Least Privilege/Fail Secure Design	n/a	n/a
Construction	Separation of duties: Coders modify only code for which they're responsible Trustworthy compilers Software evaluation tools Code review	n/a	n/a

Guidance for Addressing Malicious Code Risk

SECURITY-ENFORCING SOFTWARE cont'd

	Custom-developed	Pre-existing with Source	Pre-existing with Executable
Testing	IV&V Software evaluation tools Security testing to ensure security requirements are fulfilled. Judicious line-by-line code review Penetration testing Judicious mathematical modeling and formal verification	IV&V Software evaluation tools Security testing to ensure security requirements are fulfilled. Judicious line-by-line code review Penetration testing Judicious mathematical modeling and formal verification	n/a
Installation	Digital protection mechanisms (digital signatures, checksums, digital watermarks) Anti-tamper mechanisms (e.g., anti-tamper seals)	Digital protection mechanisms (digital signatures, checksums, digital watermarks) Anti-tamper mechanisms (e.g., anti-tamper seals)	n/a

SECURITY-RELEVANT SOFTWARE

	Custom-developed	Pre-existing with Source	Pre-existing with Executable
Acquisition	Trustworthy developers (contractor reputation) Contractor has attained CMMI Level 3 certification or equivalent Logically-closed development environment	Acquisition Policy, including: • Background checks on developer/ supplier • Trusted distribution (checksums, signatures, authenticated out of band distribution channel) • Blind buys	NIAP or FIPS evaluation, *OR* Acquisition Policy, including: • Background checks on developer/ supplier • Trusted distribution (checksums, signatures, authenticated out of band distribution channel) • Blind buys

	Custom-developed	SECURITY-RELEVANT SOFTWARE cont'd	
		Pre-existing with Source	Pre-existing with Executable
Design	Separation of duties: Designers modify only parts for which they're responsible Reputable, well-understood high-level design languages and tools.	n/a	n/a
Construction	Separation of duties: Coders modify only code for which they're responsible Software evaluation tools Code review	n/a	n/a
Testing	Security testing to ensure security requirements are fulfilled Software evaluation tools Judicious line-by-line code review	Security testing to ensure security requirements are fulfilled Software evaluation tools Judicious line-by-line code review	Security testing to ensure security requirements are fulfilled Software evaluation tools
Installation	Digital protection mechanisms (digital signatures, checksums, digital watermarks)	Digital protection mechanisms (digital signatures, checksums, digital watermarks)	Digital protection mechanisms (digital signatures, checksums, digital watermarks)

10 CONVERTING GUIDANCE INTO PROGRAM REQUIREMENTS

Because this document is considered guidance and not enforceable requirements, this section gives suggestions for incorporating the guidance into realistic programmatic requirements. The document is not intended to supersede any policy, law, or directive that is applicable to its development. Following the recommendations outlined in this document does not guarantee the software to be completely free of malicious code, but does give recommendations that will enhance the security posture if used appropriately.

The recommendations outlined in this document should be implemented in a clear and understandable fashion, so that the development organizations can account for and provide a deliverable trace of how the requirements are met. For example, if the recommendation is to perform IV&V for Scenario D, the requirement could be implemented in a software development plan stating, "All custom-developed security-enforcing software shall have an IV&V evaluation."

The recommendations may be implemented in a contractual vehicle, such as software development plans, security requirements, or an "IA Strategy" document. The set of recommendations to be incorporated need to be ultimately agreed upon by the certification and accreditation (C&A) authorities.

11 POLICIES, STANDARDS, REGULATIONS, GUIDANCE

The following standards, laws, policy, and guidance include language that addresses malicious code, software life cycle process, or software security concerns. If the referenced document is available on the World Wide Web, the URL for that document is also provided.

11.1 INTERNATIONAL STANDARDS

ISO/IEC 12207:1995, *Software Life Cycle Processes.*

ISO/IEC 17799:2005, *Information Security Standard.* Most notable is Section 10.4 "Protection against malicious and mobile code".

ISO/IEC 18028-2:2006, Network Security Architecture.

ISO/IEC 27001:2005, *Information Security Management System (ISMS) Requirements.*

ISO/IEC TR 19791:2006, *Security Assessment for Operational Systems.*

IEEE P2600/D23a, Draft Standard for Information Technology: *Hardcopy System and Device Security* (October 2006).
http://grouper.ieee.org/groups/2600/techdocs.html

11.2 FEDERAL LAWS

Title 15 United States Code (USC) Chapter 103, "Controlling the Assault of Non-Solicited Pornography and Marketing " (CAN-SPAM) (3 January 2005).
http://uscode.house.gov/download/pls/15C103.txt

Title 18 USC Part I Chapter 47 § 1030, "Fraud and related activity in connection with computers".
http://www.access.gpo.gov/uscode/title18/parti_chapter47_.html

Title 18 USC Part I Chapter 65 § 1362, "Communication lines, stations or systems" *(could be interpreted to mean that malicious code that maliciously injures or destroys, obstructs, hinders, delays, or otherwise interferes with any means of communication or transmission over said means of communication operated by the U.S., or used to support military or civil defense functions is illegal).*
http://www.access.gpo.gov/uscode/title18/parti_chapter65_.html

Title 18 USC Part I Chapter 119, "Wire and Electronic Communications Interception and Interception of Oral Communications" *(could be interpreted to mean spyware is illegal).*
http://www.access.gpo.gov/uscode/title18/parti_chapter119_.html

Title 18 USC Part I Chapter 121 § 2701, "Unlawful access to stored communications" *(could be interpreted to mean that malicious code that accesses stored communications data or records is illegal).*
http://www.access.gpo.gov/uscode/title18/parti_chapter121_.html

11.3 FEDERAL POLICY AND GUIDANCE

Office of Management and Budget (OMB) Circular No. A-130 Revised, *Management of Federal Information Resources* (28 November 2000).
http://www.whitehouse.gov/omb/circulars/a130/a130trans4.html

National Security Telecommunications and Information Systems Security Instruction (NSTISSI) No. 1000, *National Information Assurance Certification and Accreditation Process (NIACAP)* (April 2000).
http://www.cnss.gov/Assets/pdf/nstissi_1000.pdf

Mell, Peter, Karen Kent, and Joseph Nusbaum. NIST Special Publication (SP) 800-83, *Guide to Malware Incident Handling and Prevention: Recommendations of the National Institute of Standards and Technology* (November 2005).
http://csrc.nist.gov/publications/nistpubs/800-83/SP800-83.pdf

11.4 DoD POLICY AND GUIDANCE

Assistant Secretary of Defense (Network and Information Integration): *Policy Guidance for Use of Mobile Code Technologies in Department of Defense (DoD) Information Systems* (7 November 2000).
http://iase.disa.mil/mcp/index.html

DoD Directive 8100.2, *Use of Commercial Wireless Devices, Services, and Technologies in the Department of Defense (DoD) Global Information Grid (GIG)* (14 April 2004).
http://www.dtic.mil/whs/directives/corres/html/81002.htm

DoD Directive 8500.1, *Information Assurance (IA)* (24 October 2002).
http://www.dtic.mil/whs/directives/corres/html/85001.htm

DoD Instruction 8500.2, *Information Assurance (IA) Implementation* (6 February 2003).
http://www.dtic.mil/whs/directives/corres/html/85002.htm

DoD 5220.22-M, *National Industrial Security Program Operating Manual* (28 February 2006).
http://www.dtic.mil/whs/directives/corres/html/522022m.htm

DoD 5220.22-M Sup. 1, *National Industrial Security Program Operating Manual*, Supplement 1 (29 December 1994).
http://www.dtic.mil/whs/directives/corres/html/522022ms1.htm

Defense Acquisition Guidebook, Paragraph 7.5.11 "Software Security Considerations" (20 December 2004).
http://akss.dau.mil/dag/DoD5000.asp?view=document

Director of Central Intelligence Directive 6/3, *Protecting Sensitive Compartmented Information within Information Systems: Manual* (24 May 2000).
http://www.fas.org/irp/offdocs/dcid-6-3-manual.pdf or
http://www.fas.org/irp/offdocs/dcid-6-3-Manual.doc

NSA Information Assurance Solutions Technical Directors. *Information Assurance Technical Framework* (Release 3.1—September 2002).
http://www.iatf.net/framework_docs/version-3_1/index.cfm

Interim Department of Defense (DoD) Certification and Accreditation (C&A) Process Guidance. DoD Information Assurance Certification and Accreditation Process (DIACAP) (6 July 2006)[12]. http://iase.disa.mil/ditscap/interim-ca-guidance.pdf

NSA. *Information Assurance Guidance for Systems Based on a Security Real-Time Operating System.* http://www.nsa.gov/notices/notic00004.cfm?Address=/ia/government/IA_Guidance/SSE-100-1.pdf (*located at* http://www.nsa.gov/ia/government/iaGuidance.cfm?MenuID=10.3.2)

Alexander, Susan and Robert Meushaw, editors. *Trust-engineering: An Assurance Strategy for Software-based Systems*. Prepared for Dan Wolf, 22 October 2002.

11.5 SUGGESTED RESOURCES FOR FURTHER READING

Bassham, Lawrence E. and W. Timothy Polk, NIST Computer Security Division. *Threat Assessment of Malicious Code and External Attacks* (NIST Interagency Report (IR) 4939, October 1992) http://csrc.nist.gov/publications/nistir/threats/index.html

Bown, Rodney L., University of Houston-Clear Lake (for NASA Johnson Space Center Engineering Directorate Flight Data Systems Division). *Non-Developmental Item Computer Systems and the Malicious Software Threat* (April 1991) http://ntrs.nasa.gov/archive/nasa/casi.ntrs.nasa.gov/19910016319_1991016319.pdf

David A. Wheeler, Institute for Defense Analyses. *Software Configuration Management Security* (6 May 2005) http://www.dwheeler.com/essays/scm-security.html

Defense Technical Information Center (DTIC) Information Assurance Technical Analysis Center (IATAC). *Malicious Code: A State of the Art Report* (12 May 2002) http://iac.dtic.mil/iatac/reports.html

Fraunhofer Center for Research in Computer Graphics (under contract to Air Force Research Laboratory). *Final Technical Report: Mobile Code Security* (AFRL-IF-RS-TR-2004-65, March 2004) http://handle.dtic.mil/100.2/ADA422102

GAO. *Information Security: Emerging Cybersecurity Issues Threaten Federal Information Systems* (GAO-05-231, May 2005) http://www.gao.gov/cgi-bin/getrpt?GAO-05-231

GAO. *Information Security: Improving Oversight of Access to Federal Systems and Data by Contractors Can Reduce Risk* (GAO-05-362, April 2005) http://www.gao.gov/cgi-bin/getrpt?GAO-05-362

National Infrastructure Security Coordination Centre (NISCC) (United Kingdom). *Guidance on Handling Files with Possible Malicious Content* (Technical Note Id. 00147, TN03/04, 19 March 2004) http://www.niscc.gov.uk/niscc/docs/re-20040319-00147.pdf

NISCC. *The Importance of Code Signing* (Technical Note Id. 01089, TN02/2005, 14 December 2005)
http://www.niscc.gov.uk/niscc/docs/re-20051214-01089.pdf

NISCC. *Increased Use of Trojan Horse Programs* (Technical Note Id. 00080, TN01/04, 16 February 2004)
http://www.niscc.gov.uk/niscc/docs/re-20040216-00080.pdf

NISCC. *Internet Worms* (Technical Note Id. -0072, TN07/03, 05 August 2003)
http://www.niscc.gov.uk/niscc/docs/re-20030805-00727.pdf

NISCC. *Mitigating the Risk of Malicious Software* (2004)
http://www.niscc.gov.uk/niscc/docs/currentAdvice.pdf

NISCC. *Spyware* (Technical Note Id. 00384, TN04/06, 01 June 2006)
http://www.niscc.gov.uk/niscc/docs/re-20060601-00384.pdf

NISCC. *Trojan Horse Programs and Rootkits* (Technical Note Id. 00728, TN09/03, 11 September 2003)
http://www.niscc.gov.uk/niscc/docs/re-20030911-00728.pdf

NIST Computer Security Resource Center (CSRC). *Virus Information*
http://csrc.nist.gov/virus/

NIST. *Threats to Voting Systems*
http://vote.nist.gov/threats/

Philbrick, Ralph and Stephen Posniak, U.S. Equal Employment Opportunity Commission. *Procedures and Techniques for Prevention and Recovery from Fast Spreading Malware* (Virus Bulletin Conference, September 2004)
http://csrc.nist.gov/fasp/FASPDocs/incident-response/EEOCVB04PAPER.pdf

Posniak, Stephen, U.S. Equal Employment Opportunity Commission. *Combined Hardware/Software Solutions to Malware and Spam Control* (Virus Bulletin Conference, October 2005)
http://csrc.nist.gov/fasp/FASPDocs/network-security/Posniak-VB05.pdf

Radack, Shirley, NIST Computer Security Division, editor. *Preventing and Handling Malware Incidents: How to Protect Information Technology Systems from Malicious Code and Software* (*ITL Computer Security Bulletin*, December 2005)
http://www.itl.nist.gov/lab/bulletns/cslbull1.htm *or*
http://csrc.nist.gov/publications/nistbul/b-12-05.pdf

SANS Institute. *Malware FAQ* (Version 2.00—Updated August 27, 2004)
http://www.sans.org/resources/malwarefaq/

U.S. General Accountability Office (GAO). *Report to Congressional Requesters: Defense Acquisitions: Knowledge of Software Suppliers Needed to Manage Risks* (GAO-04-678, May 2004)
http://www.gao.gov/cgi-bin/getrpt?GAO-04-678

www.malware.org v.4.0
http://www.malware.org/

APPENDIX A: ABBREVIATIONS AND ACRONYMS

Table A-1 lists and amplifies all acronyms and abbreviations used in this document.

Table A-1: Abbreviations and Acronyms

Acronym or Abbreviation	Amplification
AIS	Automated Information System
C&A	Certification and Accreditation
CAS	Center for Assured Software
CERT	Computer Emergency Readiness Team
CM	Configuration Management
CMMI	Capability Maturity Model-Integrated
CNSS	The Committee for National Security Systems
COTS	Commercial Off-The-Shelf
DAA	Designated Approving authority
DCID	Director of Central Intelligence Directive
DHS	Department of Homeland Security
DoD	Department of Defense
FIPS	Federal Information Processing Standard
GIG	Global Information Grid
GOTS	Government Off-The-Shelf
IA	Information Assurance
IAD	Information Assurance Directorate
IDE	Integrated Development Environment
IEEE/EIA	Institute of Electrical and Electronics Engineers/Electronic Industries Association
ISSE	Information System Security Engineer
IT	Information Technology
IV&V	Independent Validation and Verification
JWICS	Joint Worldwide Intelligence Communications System
MOTS	Modified Off-The-Shelf
NCSC-TG	National Computer Security Center - Technical Guide
NIAP	National Information Assurance Partnership
NIPRNet	Non-Classified Internet Protocol Router Network
NIST	National Institute of Standards and Technology
NSA	National Security Agency

Acronym or Abbreviation	Amplification

NSS	National Security System
OSS	Open Source Software
PKI	Public Key Infrastructure
RUP	Rational Unified Process
SAMATE	Software Assurance Metrics And Tool Evaluation
SAR	Special Access Required
SCI	Sensitive Compartmented Information
SCM	Software Configuration Management
SEI	Security Engineering Institute
SIPRNet	Secret Internet Protocol Router Network
SPICE	Software Process Improvement Capability
SQL	Structured Query Language
SSE	Systems Security Engineering
URL	Uniform Resource Locators
US	United States
XML	eXtensible Markup Language

APPENDIX B: REFERENCES

The following are resources referenced throughout this document, listed alphabetically by author (individual or organization). When a resource is available on the World Wide Web, its URL is provided.

- Alexander, Susan and Robert Meushaw, editors. *Trust-Engineering: An Assurance Strategy for Software-Based Systems.* Prepared for Dan Wolf, 22 October 2002.

- Committee for National Security Systems Instruction (CNSSI) 4009. *National Information Assurance (IA) Glossary.* Revised June 2006.
  http://www.cnss.gov/Assets/pdf/cnssi_4009.pdf

- Department of Defense Directive (DODD) 8500.1, *Information Assurance (IA).* 24 October 2002.
  http://www.dtic.mil/whs/directives/corres/html/85001.htm

- Director of Central Intelligence. Directive 6/3, *Protecting Sensitive Compartmented Information within Information Systems—Manual.*
  http://www.fas.org/irp/offdocs/DCID_6-3_20Manual.htm

- F.O.C.U.S.ed Enterprises. IEEE 12207 *"Software Life Cycle Processes": Introduction for the Implementation of Software Configuration Management.* Dated January 2005; Presented at the National Defense Industrial Association 2005 Technical Information Division Annual Conference, Miami, Florida, 3-4 March 2005.
  http://www.dtic.mil/ndia/2005techinfo/12207.ppt

- Goertzel, Karen Mercedes, *et al.* (for the DHS NCSD). *Security in the Software Life Cycle: Making Software Processes—and the Software Produced by Them—More Secure.* Draft Version 1.2, August 2006.
  https://buildsecurityin.us-cert.gov/daisy/bsi/87.html?branch=1&language=1

- Grance, Tim, Joan Hash, and Marc Stevens. Special Publication 800-64 Rev. 1, *Security Considerations in the Information System Development Life Cycle: Recommendations of the National Institute of Standards and Technology.* Revision 1, June 2004.
  http://csrc.nist.gov/publications/nistpubs/800-64/NIST-SP800-64.pdf

- Hoglund, Greg, and Gary McGraw. *Exploiting Software: How to Break Code.* Addison-Wesley, 2004.

- Moore, James W. *Mapping the "Malcode" Outline to the "NDIA Document": Preliminary Analysis.* Draft 1, 7 September 2006.

- National Computer Security Center (NCSC). Technical Guide (TG) 006, *A Guide to Understanding Configuration Management in Trusted Systems.* NCSC-TG-006/Library No. S-228,590, 28 March 1988.
  http://www.radium.ncsc.mil/tpep/library/rainbow/NCSC-TG-006.pdf

- National Computer Security Center (NCSC). Technical Guide 008, *A Guide to Understanding Trusted Distribution in Trusted Systems.* NCSC-TG-008/Library No. S-

228,592, 15 December 1988.
http://www.radium.ncsc.mil/tpep/library/rainbow/NCSC-TG-008.pdf

- NSA CAS. *Software Assurance Glossary*. Draft, 11 October 2006

- NSA Information Assurance Solutions Technical Directors. *Information Assurance Technical Framework (IATF)*. Release 3.1, September 2002.
  http://www.iatf.net/framework_docs/version-3_1/index.cfm

- Pauli, J. and D. Xu. Threat-Driven Architectural Design of Secure Information Systems. In *Proceedings of the International Conference on Information Systems (ICEIS'05)*, 2005.

- Reeves, J.W. "Code as Design: Three Essays by Jack W. Reeves". in *Developer.*: The Independent Magazine for Software Developers*, 23 February 2005.
  http://www.developerdotstar.com/mag/articles/PDF/DevDotStar_Reeves_CodeAsDesign.pdf

- Sun Microsystems. *A Patch Management Strategy for the Solaris Operating Environment*. Prentice Hall Professional Technical Reference, 23 May 2003.
  http://www.phptr.com/articles/article.asp?p=31760&seqNum=2&rl=1

- Tipton, Harold F. and Kevin Henry, editors. *Official (ISC)² Guide to the CISSP Common Body of Knowledge*. Auerbach, November 2006.

ENDNOTES

[1] Goertzel, Karen Mercedes, *et al.* (for the DHS NCSD). *Security in the Software Life Cycle: Making Software Processes—and the Software Produced by Them—More Secure.* Draft Version 1.2, August 2002.

[2] Software Process Subgroup of the Task Force on Security Across the Software Development Life Cycle. *Procesess to Produce Secure Software.* National Cyber Security Summit, March 2004.

[3] Pauli, J. and D. Xu. "Threat-Driven Architectural Design of Secure Information Systems". In *Proceedings of the International Conference on Information Systems (ICEIS'05)*, 2005.

[4] Alexander, Susan and Robert Meushaw, editors. *Trust-Engineering: An Assurance Strategy for Software-Based Systems.* Prepared for Dan Wolf, 22 October 2002.

[5] Goertzel, *et al. Security in the Software Life Cycle,* Appendix G:G.6.1.1.9. "Insecure Installation".

[6] F.O.C.U.S.ed Enterprises. *IEEE 12207 Software Life Cycle Processes: Introduction for the Implementation of Software Configuration Management.* January 2005, presented at National Defense Industrial Association 2005 Technical Information Division Annual Conference, Miami, Florida, 3-4 March 2005. Also James W. Moore. *Mapping the "Malcode" Outline to the "NDIA Document": Preliminary Analysi*s. Draft 1, 7 September 2006.

[7] National Security Agency Information Assurance Solutions Technical Directors. *Information Assurance Technical Framework (IATF).* Release 3.1, September 2002.

[8] Tipton, Harold F. and Kevin Henry, editors. *Official (ISC)² Guide to the CISSP CBK.* Auerbach, November 2006.

[9] *ibid.*

[10] *ibid.*

[11] Sun Microsystems. *A Patch Management Strategy for the Solaris Operating Environment.* Prentice Hall Professional Technical Reference, 23 May 2003.

[12] The IA section of the draft updated *Defense Acquisition Guidebook,* which includes a revised discussion of software security considerations (Section 8.4.3) is currently available for review at: https://acc.dau.mil/CommunityBrowser.aspx?id=31651